THE PINNACLE OF INDIAN THOUGHT

Several centuries before Christ there lived in India a great sage, Shankarāchārya, whose memory is still revered because of his profound wisdom and his exposition of the Vedic teachings. His best known work was the *Viveka Chūdāmani* (Crest Jewel of Discrimination or Crest Jewel of Wisdom), a Sanskrit classic which has endured through the centuries because of its depth of wisdom and truth. Although this work has been translated many times into English and there are numerous commentaries, this new translation and commentary by Professor Ernest Wood is particularly valuable because he was a Western scholar who spent many years in the East. Therefore he has been able to translate the profound concepts of ancient Indian thought into language that may be followed without difficulty by the Western reader.

The author was born in England and educated in the field of science. As a young man he went to India where he spent many years as an educationist, serving as principal of various schools, colleges and universities, and also as a worker for the world-wide Theosophical Society. Professor Wood became deeply interested in the Yoga and Vedanta philosophies of India and has written many books on these subjects, as well as on education and psychology. After leaving India he was for some time President and then Dean of the American Academy of Asian Studies, a graduate school in San Francisco.

THE PINNACLE OF INDIAN THOUGHT

Being a new, independent translation
of the Viveka Chūdāmani
(Crest Jewel of Discrimination)
with commentaries.

ERNEST WOOD

A QUEST BOOK
Published under a grant from The Kern Foundation

THE THEOSOPHICAL PUBLISHING HOUSE
Wheaton, Ill., U.S.A.
Madras, India / London, England

Away with those that preach to us the washing off of sin—
Thine own self is the stream for thee to make ablutions in:
In self-restraint it rises pure—flows clear in tide of truth,
By widening banks of wisdom, in waves of peace and truth.
Bathe there, thou son of Pandu! with reverence and rite,
For never yet was water wet could wash the spirit white.

—*The Book of Good Counsels (Hitopadesa)*
translated by Edwin Arnold

PUBLISHER'S NOTE

Professor Wood has translated the Sanskrit work entitled *Viveka-Chūdāmani* as "The Crest-Jewel of Discrimination." This stresses the motif running through Shankarāchārya's text. However, it should be stated that the work is best known under the title used by many translators, namely *The Crest-Jewel of Wisdom*.

INTRODUCTORY NOTE

While preparing the manuscript of *The Pinnacle of Indian Thought* for the printers, it was noticed that there were variant spellings in Sanskrit words as well as in orthography. Because of this the publishers requested the undersigned to look over the manuscript and systematize the spellings, and this has accordingly been done. It should be mentioned, however, that there are several methods of anglicizing Sanskrit words, especially so in connection with the sibilants, of which there are three in Sanskrit. Professor Wood preferred using but two modes of distinguishing the sibilants: that of the hard-sound "s" (as in the word "us") and the soft sound "sh" (as in the word "hush"). Thus he utilized the spelling of Shankarāchārya in place of Sankarāchārya, and sharīra instead of sarīra (which system was followed in his *Yoga Dictionary*). He also utilized the makron, indicating a lengthening in the sound-value of vowels, in place of the circumflex accent. This method is also followed herein.

Along with his translation, Professor Wood placed a number at the beginning of each verse, to which he refers from time to time in his commentary. It will be noticed that he did not translate all of the original Sanskrit verses. His numbering is not the same as that used by other translators.

It may be observed that āchārya signifies "teacher"; thus Shankarāchārya signifies "Shankara, the teacher."

Geoffrey A. Barborka

CONTENTS

CHAPTER 1

INTRODUCTION TO THE FOUR QUALIFICATIONS

The first thirty verses of this famous Sanskrit classic of Shankarāchārya is the handbook of many of the intellectuals of India, used for guidance in their daily religious life. It bases itself upon a section of the Vedas which aims at being informative in the main, while other sections are more in the nature of tradition and worship. The entire booklet of 580 verses is entitled Viveka Chūdāmani — literally "Crest-jewel of Discrimination," for Chūdāmani means a jewel (mani) worn on the top (chūdā) of the head or turban, and viveka means, according to a leading Sanskrit dictionary (Apte's), "the power of distinguishing between the visible world and the invisible spirit, or of separating reality from mere semblance or illusion." Sometimes, incidentally, a person competent to expound this subject is called by his followers a swan (hansa), in reference to an old story in which the swan is credited with the ability to take milk from a mixture of milk and water.

Chūdā is also the lock of hair on the very top of the head, and mani is a jewel worn in that position, so this expression tells us that discernment (viveka) is the best of all knowledge. It is the title of a famous book by Shankarāchārya, one of the most famous writers of old India, on the subject of the most important teaching of the Vedas, the Vedānta. That teaching is not a set of dogmas, but an inspiration to direct perception of the most important thing in life, which is the true or real Self, to be distinguished from the erroneous self-images which we make from time to time.

I have endeavored to make a "matter-of-fact" translation, keeping very close to the original text, but avoiding foreign idioms and sentence-form, and condensing (for saving space) where there is too much repetition (beloved of the Eastern mind) or too foreign or unnecessary or too lurid an illustration, but leaving out no informative idea.

The book opens with an act of reverence, as was customary: —

> *Verse 1*. I bow devoutly to Govinda, supreme joy and teacher of truth, who is the subject and purpose of all the high teachings of the Vedas, but himself has no limits.

Govinda is one of the many appellations of the Supreme Deity. It comes from the belief that Shrī Krishna was a special incarnation of Deity, coming down into human form for the benefit of mankind to restore goodness when it was on the decline. This incarnation is traditionally held to have taken place about five thousand years ago. A part of the story of Krishna is that when he was a boy he lived in the country and part of his occupation was looking after the cows. The term is extended also to the idea that the "cows" are the verses of the holy scriptures (Vedas) and the Deity is the caretaker of them.

It is notable that in the dedicatory first verse of many of his writings Shankara lays emphasis on God as the supreme teacher — in this case, teacher of truth or reality. To Shankara the Supreme Deity is the source of all inspiration and true knowledge, while the intellect is supreme in its own realm — the outside world.

Verses 2 to 10 are preparatory to the main purpose of the early part of the Chūdāmani, the chief value of which to most people lies in its description of the character or qualities which we humans must develop in ourselves in order to be able to aim intelligently at an understanding of God and man and the relation between them. Without such self-education we cannot hope to look even at ourselves without terrible distortion, much less to understand the meaning of God (Brahman). The description of the "qualifications" required begins at verse 17 but is preceded by some introductory material in verses 11 to 16. To save space I will now summarize verses 2 to 10:

> Birth as a human being is not a trivial matter, therefore do not be such a fool as to throw your opportunity away. Especially is this so if you have an inclination for philosophic studies. Otherwise you may wander for many lives without achieving any real purpose, or freedom from this present sort of life, which is bondage. Scripture, sacrifices, rituals, worship, wealth, works and words will not release you — you must yourself discover your own real identity. This can be done only by observation and thought. The words of scripture and wise teachers will help — but only if you use them to ponder and reason upon. By all means seek guidance from gurus, men who appear to have themselves discovered the reality, and to be living accordingly.

Still, verses 11 to 16 present some safeguards, before we proceed to the real business of the four "qualifications."

Beginning with verse 11 we find a description of the difference between doing and knowing. Doing is for external purposes, knowing for internal. This does not apply to the lower knowing, which means knowledge about doing (what things are and how to use them), but to the higher knowing, which means knowledge about the nature of our being. The

I or self must be intimately known, by oneself and in one-self, and not by any comparison with anything else. In modern science we have had statements of belief in the "indestructibility of matter," and the "conservation of energy." Of these two beliefs the first broke down when the atom was dissected and it became the belief that matter was only energy or force in a certain condition. The teaching we are now considering goes one step further and says all actions whether of body or mind and their products are only the expression of a certain condition of life, which is equated to consciousness. Thus it is not external things that condition us, but it is we who have made and are making those things. There is an immense amount of those things because there is an immense quantity of us; by "us" is meant consciousness in the sub-human orders of nature as well as in the human. This verse reads:

> *Verse 11.* Karma (work or action, including "good works") is for the purification of the mind (chitta), not for obtaining the real. The accomplishment of realization (vastu-siddhi) is by means of considering, not at all by tens of millions of actions.

Now we come to the qualifications: —

Verse 12 then proceeds to compare this with the familiar analogy of the rope and the snake — the example of a seeming snake which on proper inspection is found to be only a piece of rope. In arriving at the truth we have the help of others in that we can consider the views of philosophers and seers, just as we have the help of others in the field of actions or works, such as food, clothing, shelter and education. But:

> *Verse 13.* Certainty of the truth is seen by means of considering the beneficial declarations, not by bathings, donations or hundreds of breathing practices.

Verse 14. The fruition depends upon the qualified (or competent) person. In this, place, time, etc. are only incidentals.

Verse 15 then emphasizes that one who desires to realize the truth of the self should practice "consideration," with the help of a guru, who is called an "ocean of compassion" and has the ultimate knowledge of Brahman. The seeking and following of learned and saintly men, and consideration of their views with the deepest respect, was much spoken of in the old days, when few were literate and books on this subject were only beginning to be written by pioneers such as Shankarāchārya. Our text does not recommend the decadent idea that one must go to a guru to be told what to believe. On the contrary, verse 16 states that the "qualified person" has to be an intelligent man, learned, and capable of arguing pros and cons. In short, he must have four qualifications, which we now find enumerated in verses 17 and 18:

Verse 17. It is considered that the desire to know Brahman is suitable only for a person having (1) discrimination, (2) detachment, (3) calmness and five other attainments, and (4) desire for liberation.

Verse 18. It is stated by the wise in this connection that these four practices are essential for those good people, and that without them there is no success.

Verse 19. (1) Firstly, the discrimination between what is constant and what is fleeting is to be considered. (2) Next to that is uncoloredness (or unaffectedness) by anticipated enjoyments in this world or elsewhere. (3) Next come the six attainments beginning with calmness of mind (shama), and (4) the desire for liberation. These are made very clear.

These "four qualifications" or practices will now be more precisely described: —

> *Verse 20.* (1) That Brahman is the reality (or truth) and that the world is false is the definite formulation. This is described as discrimination between what is constant and what is fleeting.

Without some ultimate reality or power to be, there could not be anything. In the doctrine of materialism it was held that matter as known to the senses was this ultimate self-existent reality. When this idea received a severe blow at the hands of the physicists who split the atom and showed it to be constituted of "forces" the idea arose that "forces" or "energies" are the basis of reality and that matter is only materials compacted from or by these. Yet one prominent scientist could say that even so "the world looks more like a great mind than a great machine." This paves the way for theories of mind or life or consciousness as paramount and basic. In this view the world is manufactured or is, if you like the word, *ersatz*. Even the thinking mind is to be included in this collection of false-nesses, for it is clear — is it not? — that even that mind itself is governed by rules or laws of logic, and must submit to those laws, which are more basic than its products or ideas. Thus it is not itself independent or basic, but is a manufactured tool, an instrument for use, just as a spade is used for digging.

What then of the ideas of God (Brahman) and of liberation? These are not ideas arrived at by the thinking mind, but are of the nature of illumination, intuition or insight. There are words which convey this distinction — for *manas* indicates the thinking mind, and *buddhi* indicates the discerning or illuminated mind. In this way the senses, or rather sensation, is nearer to reality than is reasoning or inference, for reasoning is based upon "something known" through the senses, and is thus a means for checking the accuracy of sense-perceptions or for discovery of the unseen. Even so, *buddhi* is only a half-way house to the truth, for *buddhi* is the discovery and perception of "others" and the acceptance of them, which is love of them, as distinguished from the discovery and acceptance of mere things by *manas,* and its "love" of them, which is mental interest.

Beyond even *buddhi,* then, is what we are seeking in our present study, and it, in this series of words is ātmā (ātman), one's own very being, or better, the very being that is oneself.

Reviewing this collection that we call "the world," we are trying to find what is self-dependent. This is a time process. The babe first knows itself only. It is not only conscious, but is consciousness conscious of itself. Next it finds the outside world. Next it finds itself (mistakenly) to be part of that world, by identification. Then it finds others (other selves) as parts of the world. The identification of oneself and others with the world is an error. It is the mistaking of the spade for the man. It is not that the earth and the spade must be denied. Let them be seen and used, but let the man *also* be seen. And in this matter of knowing what we are, let not only the mind be seen, but let the consciousness *also* be seen, and seen as such, as what it is, regardless of what the body and the mind, the earth and the spade, are. One beginning this study is a spade thinking itself to be a man (very funny), or a mind thinking itself to be a self. The earth is so muddy, so viscous that the spade comes up all covered with the sticky stuff, and must be cleaned (or cleared, if a mind) before it can dig well. This is where the qualification called discrimination (viveka) comes in. It is the clarification of the situation. It is not the actual discovery of the self. It is one of the group of four qualifications for undertaking the discovery.

Verse 20 speaks of Brahman, not Atman. But other verses will state that the two are one. One who knows the one knows both. Only one who knows the "God within oneself" knows what God is, and the unity of God and the real man. As Emerson saw it: "There is no bar or wall in the soul where man leaves off and God begins." In the progress of religions in the world, men keep on formulating a better God, according to their own best. Men build their gods according to what they are or what they have become. Thus "God Almighty," as "The smith a mighty man was he, with strong and sinewy arms." Thus man as he advances builds himself a better God, and the logical conclusion of this will be that when man is perfect his God also will be perfect, and the two will be one.

We come now to verse 21, which speaks of the second qualification: —

> *Verse 21.* Detachment (vairāgya) is the putting away of all that is seen, or heard, etc. — all objects of enjoyment (or sense), which are certainly temporary, from those of the body up to the manifest Deity.

I have often written on this topic,* so will be as brief as possible here. Generally I have translated the word as "uncoloredness" (vai = against, and rāgya = being colored). It has the same sense as "being conditioned." Of course, all of us to a large extent follow social customs, and all kinds of habits, but there is or should be something and some activity in our lives which represents current living. Briefly, we have to see that our lives are not governed by circumstances, whatever happens, we should consciously decide what to do about it — whether we lose everything or inherit a million dollars, it is all the same in this respect. So vairāgya (detachment or

---

*Vide *Practical Yoga: Ancient and Modern,* Dutton and Co., New York, 1948, and *Yoga,* Penguin Books, England, 1959.

uncoloredness) does not mean suppression of body, feelings or mind, but positive use of these, as if they were spades.

We now come to a verse describing the six attainments or accomplishments.

> *Verse 22.* The state of control of the mind (manas), when it is detached from the assemblage of external objects as a result of observation again and again of their defects, is called calmness (shama).

Here, of course, is meant the power and habit of keeping the mind quiet when it is not being used. This does not suggest suppression of the mind. It is needed for living in this world. The case is similar to that of the body — its legs and arms must not start jigging about or going for a walk on their own account, but must remain quiet when not ordered otherwise. In this connection there are practices of keeping it quiet or relaxing it for short periods, just to gain the conscious control. Thought obeys the will, that is, you can think about what *you* choose. What the will is will be considered later, but we may note here that it is not the same as thought.

We come now, in the next verse, to two more of the accomplishments: —

> *Verse 23.* The turning away of both kinds of bodily organs (those of sensation, hearing, etc., and those of action, hands and feet, etc.) from their respective sense-objects is proclaimed to be control of body (dama).

It is a fact, of course, that we as conscious beings do not carry on our living in the body as such, but in what are called the ten organs (five of sense for reception of impressions from the outside world, and five of action for affecting the world). It is not suggested that these should be suppressed but that they should be quiet when not in use. There are many occasions on which we all do not pay attention to the message of the senses, as, for example, when we are reading an interesting book, someone may come into the room in full view and not be noticed. Here the attention is withdrawn from the senses, but our present verse speaks of the turning away of the senses. I take this to be the discouragement of their natural tendency to watch what is going on (in the case of the sense-organs) and to be restless (in the case of the action-organs). This is largely a matter of habit.

> *Verse 23 (b).* The non-dependence of the mental activities (vrittis) upon externals is the best abstention (uparati).

Here we come again to our previous distinction between living for living and living for enjoyment of objects. It is important that external objects should not govern our lives, but that we should *use* them for *our* purposes. In this connection it is often mentioned that depending upon external rites and ceremonies is to be avoided. All this is in contrast to the way in which most people look to externals for something to depend upon, when they might better have some purposes of their own, except when there is need for a change and some diversion.

> *Verse 24.* The bearing of all afflictions without discontent or any resentment and without anxiety or complaint — that is declared to be endurance.

This is part of the philosophy of non-antagonism — accepting all that comes and assessing impartially its value and the opportunity it offers for the building of character.

> *Verse 25.* The careful and accurate understanding of the truth and wisdom of the scriptures and the words of the

guru — that is proclaimed by the sages to be the faith by
which the reality is experienced.

It may be noted that the word usually translated faith (i.e.
shraddhā) might better be translated confidence — confidence
in the ideas being studied, and also confidence in one's own
ability to understand. Allied to this is the meaning of the
word often translated teacher (i.e. guru). It means literally
"weighty," and therefore worthy of most careful consideration. Reverence, veneration and worship are extreme applica-
tions of this idea. It is a part of advanced practical philosophy
to see that *all* experiences are worthy of reverence.

> *Verse 26.* Constant establishing of the understanding in
> the always pure Brahman is called unified poise
> (samādhāna), not the play of the idea-mind (chitta).

There is stress here upon the *deep* understanding of Brahman as the subject of the *poise* of the mind. It must become
the habit of the mind, so that, having *thought* all it can about
Brahman it may find itself in that eager poised condition
beyond thought in which an intuition from above — or as
Shankara would probably put it, from beyond all this — may
bring an illuminating realization, which presents everything
as in that unity beyond any of the previously thought-of
categories. We have now completed the six attainments.

Next comes the last of the four qualifications: —

> *Verse 27.* The desire for freedom (mumukshutva) is
> the determination (ichchhā) to free oneself, by one's
> own awareness of one's own real nature, from the
> bondages produced by ignorance (or error) beginning
> with egoism and ending with the body.

It is to be noted here that the freedom referred to is not
freedom from external things but from the coverings and

instruments of one's essential self, not from the earth, so to speak, but from the spade. An instance within my experience is that of the principal of a psychiatry college here in America who, when he alluded to himself in class as a doctor, was challenged by a visiting professor with the statement that he was not a doctor. He was startled until it was explained that the doctor that he seemed to be, though a real doctor, and an eminent one, was only one of his "spades," while he — the real being that he was — was always consciously present when using the spades. The determination or resolution to realize this truth fully and not to lose sight of it is the fourth qualification. This is by no means a vague desire, but a definite piece of conscious work. Even if it is only mild, adds the next verse, 28, it can grow through the practice of the second and third qualifications.

Verse 29 then informs us that in the case of one in whom both the detachment and the desire for liberation are strong, calmness and the others of its group soon become very meaningful and fruitful. On the other hand, (verse 30) if both detachment and the desire for liberation are feeble, calmness and the rest of the six attainments "water but the desert."

CHAPTER 2

VARIOUS PARTS OF MAN

I begin now in what we may call the second part of the book at verse 71, in which the teacher tells the student about the various parts of man. Although the text is replete with interesting points we shall have very little room for comments, so I will put in no explanation of my own except occasionally in parentheses. The first part, up to verse 70, will be dealt with only later, as it contains mostly advice about the attitude which the student should take up and why he should study at all; this most of our readers might regard with some impatience. We will proceed with the informative part of the work. A guru is now supposed to be speaking to a pupil or enquirer.

71. I will now tell you what ought to be known. Having heard this correctly, you must understand it in yourself.

72-3. This body (of ours) is an aggregate of bones, fat, flesh, etc., using limbs and parts such as arms, chest and head. It is a seat of foolishness, announced as "I" or "mine."

73-4. There are five subtle (very fine or invisible) elements (conditions of matter), named solid, liquid, fiery (with heat), aery (gaseous) and skyey (etheric). These five, compounded together (in the proportion of 50 percent of one of them to 12½ percent of each of the other four), become dense (no longer subtle), and constitute the matter of the dense body. Their own natures (i.e. the subtle, called tanmātras) become objective as five, the sound, feeling, sight, taste and smell of things, for the pleasure of the enjoyer (subject).

75-8. Those foolish people who are attached to the objects come and go, up and down, carried by their own actions. But he who is free from the lure of sense-object — so difficult to avoid — he is fit for liberation (mukti). Not so any other, even though he be learned in all the six sciences.

79-80. Those who are only superficially desirous of liberation from the ocean of objective existence are caught by desires and sunk in the middle of the way. But he who has killed the crocodile (or is it shark?) of sense-objects with the sword of good non-attachment (or, literally, not-being-colored) goes to the other shore without any obstruction.

81. He whose understanding is not good, going by the rough roads of objects (i.e., with objective aims) meets only with (repeated) death, but he who proceeds with the advice of a helpful and good guru (teacher), in conjunction with his own, attains success. You should know this as true.

82-7. If you really have a desire for liberation, shun the sense-object (motive or aim) from a distance, as though it were poison, and always choose with loving care the nectar-bearing virtues of contentment, compassion, patient forgiveness, sincerity, tranquillity, and self-control. Choose emancipation from ignorance. The body is for the sake of others. He who is attached to it is committing (spiritual) suicide. It is like crossing a river on a crocodile, mistaking it for a log of wood. Conquer all infatuations, and so go to the supreme state of Vishnu.

88. This dense body, formed by past karma (actions) from the compounded dense materials, is one's basis for enjoyment. From this arises the waking state, with its experience of dense objects.

89-90. The liv-er (jīva) then pays attention to the classes of dense things, by means of the outer organs of sense and action, by self-identification with this (body), and from this comes a favorable appraisal of this body, in the waking state. This dense body, then, which is now the basis for all the outer affairs (sansara) of the indwelling spirit (purusha), becomes, as it were, the home of this householder.

91. There it is, then, with all its qualifications — its births, age and death, its bulkiness, etc. (figure) of various kinds, its conditions such as infancy, etc., its obligations of social caste and stages of life, its meeting with reverence or contumely or high esteem — various indeed.

92. On account of knowing about things there are the organs of knowledge (i.e. senses), ears (for hearing), skin (for touch), eyes (for seeing), tongue (for taste) and nose (for smell). By inclination to act there are the organs of action — vocal organs, hands, feet, and organs for elimination and generation.

The next part will deal with the mind and its constituents, vitality, waking, dreaming and sleeping states, illusion, etc.

93 (a). The inner instrument (i.e., mind) is spoken of as mentality (manas), higher intelligence (buddhi), and individuality (ahankriti, i.e., "I-creation"), with their revolvements (vrittis, i.e., courses of activity).

Comment. The previous verses described the main constituents of the *body*. Now comes the *mind*. Notice the order of the thought in this verse: The mind (antahkarana, i.e., "inner instrument" of the living being, as distinguished from the body, which is an outer instrument) contains four functions. It is not that we think of these four things and then say that the mind is a collective name for the four. On the contrary, here we think first of the mind as one fact (which is directly perceived by us in ourselves by some means other than the senses, for it cannot be sensed by ears, eyes, skin, tongue or nose) and regard it as *one* fact, the inner or invisible or not-objective part or means of our living. The second half of verse 93 and the whole of 94, which now follow, define the four functions of the mind:

93 (b). Mentality (manas) is planning, wondering, etc. (about objects).

93 (c). Higher intelligence (buddhi) is the characteristic of placing (things of all kinds) in (their) categories.

94 (a). Entifying (ahankriti) is "saying I," on account of self-regard.

94 (b). The outgoing mentality (chitta) is characterized by the quality of seeking after one's own (material) good.

Comment. The classifying of facts reaches a high point when buddhi observes and feels the distinction between living and non-living, and evaluates things accordingly. Mentality (manas) may be regarded as concerned with the mental manipulation of *objects,* along with its form of interest in the same (a wide range from games of mental skill to the problems of the world of life). Higher intelligence (buddhi) has its interest in the *life* around and in us. Next comes recognition of and interest in *self* (ahankriti or ahankāra). Chitta, the fourth, is *mere* recognition and memory of objects, without thought about them (as in animals), that is, without reasoning about them or planning to change them. It collects and stores sense-experiences as mental images. It is said to contain five kinds of ideas, which it classifies as (1) correct ideas (e.g., "the earth is a spinning ball"), (2) wrong ideas (e.g., "the moon is made of green cheese"), (3) imaginings, (4) dreams, (5) memories.

In the foregoing we have brief statements as to what the four divisions or functions of the mind are. They have definite designations: *manas* for the thinking and inquiring part of it (rationality, logicality, inference); *buddhi* for the observation of classes or categories (including the very fundamental or basic distinction between the mind and the body, or the living and the non-living); ahankāra or ahankriti for saying I. Psychologically, this saying of I, or regarding oneself as an individual, applies in two ways — to self-identity and also to regarding other things as individuals or separate objects. To make the distinction clearer between the first three functions and the fourth I may remark that the animal mind merely observes and recognizes things without reasoning about them (so the chitta is lower mind, including memory to the extent of recognition of things when they are seen), whereas the human mind (manas) plans to investigate and alter them, and when superior (buddhi) it sees the usefulness of things *for the purpose of life*. So buddhi is often translated as wisdom, while chitta and manas are merely knowing and thinking. It may also be noted that chitta or lower mind includes *desires* and *aversions* with regard to the recognized objects, based upon former pleasures and pains derived from them. It was therefore remarked by Patañjali that all ideas (thoughts of things) are either pleasant or unpleasant, which is another way of saying that there is no thought without feeling.

The "inner instrument" (antahkarana) or total mind has been described in verses 93 and 94. Our author now, in verse 95, speaks of *vitality* as another part of the human being, and also states that this works along five main lines in the body. These five are simply listed, but no definitions or descriptions are given:

> 95. The vitality (prāna) becomes breathing, elimination, circulation, procreation and digestion, according to modifications of function and form — just as gold, water, etc. (have various forms).

Comment. The idea in this verse is that these five functions, which seem to be found in some form in all animal bodies (and perhaps even in plants) are caused by the invisible prāna (vitality) and not by any *material* combination, so they constitute "the life of the body." That the same one vitality appears in these same five forms in most if not all living organisms suggests a sort of "vitality spectrum" operating similarly in all.

We come now in verses 96 and 97 to a further statement about the part of man that is beyond the body, well known to us but not known through the bodily senses:

> 96. What is called "the subtle body" is an eight-fold city (i.e., organism):
> (1) the five beginning with speech,
> (2) the five beginning with hearing,
> (3) the five beginning with breathing,
> (4) the five headed by sky-matter,
> (5) higher intelligence (buddhi) etc., (the four),
> (6-8) ignoring (avidyā), desire, and doing actions.

Comment. These are in other words (1) the five kinds of action, (2) the five kinds of sensing, (3) the five functions of vitality, (4) the five forms of *conditions* of matter, (5) the four-fold inner instrument, (6) the limitation by which we deal with *portions* of reality only — i.e., the relativity-limitation, which involves and is involved with (7) specific desires and (8) specific doings or actions.

It is interesting, in view of modern scientific discovery beyond our earth's atmosphere, that the five conditions of matter were listed as according to solidity, liquidity, temperature, vaporousness *and* "skyness" (often translated as "etheric"). Would we be wrong in calling these the five functions of materiality, analagous to the five functions of vitality? More light will be thrown on this by the theory of *five-fold subdivision* mentioned in verse 97.

> 97. This subtle-body—listen (carefully)—known also as the character (linga)—body, composed of the five *unmixed* materials, together with habitual tendencies (vāsanās), and having the experience of the results of actions, is a beginningless deceptive appearance (upādhi) of the Self.

Comment. Character means what the man *is* in his mind, as distinguished from the dense or physical body, which is what the mind *uses*. It is to be noticed that a man *is* what he *does*, and all the items mentioned in verse 96 are forms of "doing." There is such a thing, for example, as the doing of thinking — "What are you doing?" "Just thinking." What a person is at any given time presents only a portion of his character; thus a man may be a motorist, a carpenter, a husband, a drunkard, etc., but not all at once. Myself — I find myself putting down my pen every now and then, and just thinking or even mentally gazing. It is all "doing." Even the deepest meditation is not a state, but a doing.

It is here that we can see the difference between the "unmixed materials" of the subtle body and the mixed materials of the world of the dense body. The latter is said to be composed of five-fold-compounded (Pañchikarana) material. Pure unmixed material is of the nature of doing ("creation" means doing). The five-fold mixing of materials can be described as follows. Take any solid, such as, let us say, a piece of iron. It is half-solid, one-eighth liquid, one-eighth of temperature, one-eighth gaseous and one-eighth skyey or etheric. All the five are there in some degree. Chemical "decomposition" could be studied in the light of this "fiving" — not assuming, of course, that the proportions are always the same. Also it may have to do with the irreconcilability of wave-theory and corpuscle-theory, and the relations, e.g., between heat and light.

When the subtle body is called a "deceptive appearance" it does not mean delusion; this "upādhi" is a fact, but it is not *oneself* and does not present oneself, but is only a tool or instrument.

A point here is that the subtle "world" differs from the dense world in that in the former the five kinds of matter are pure or unmixed, and have their own doing-nature, not arrested or halted by compromise. I have in years past made considerable study of the facts of tested clairvoyance, and have found that the forms of the "astral plane" are all expressions of emotions (not of actions), and the forms of the "mental plane" are all "thought-forms," etc. That means they are *not actions,* but their matter is not *action-matter,* so that to regard it as only "finer matter, but *like* our physical matter" is an erroneous supposition. We do not know, or know of, any fundamental material building-blocks or plastic negative substance on any plane. There really are no "planes" but only habitats (no talas, but only lokas). Thinking of *planes* is really materialist philosophy. Thinking of *worlds,* in which the objects are, so to say, frozen actions, frozen emotions, frozen thoughts, etc., is logical and realistic. It is clear, is it not, that our bodies are frozen actions, that is, they consist of structures and functions which have become such by long habit.

We come next to an explanation of the dream-state:

> 98 (a). Dream is a particular state of this (subtle body), in which it shines (manifests) by residues of itself merely (with no outside world).

> 98 (b). Now, in dream the intelligence (buddhi) is itself alone, with impressions (vāsanās) of various kinds of the (prior) waking state coming up for the time being.

Comment. This statement is about the dream state and is rather surprisingly close in line with our modern thought of the subconscious mind, in which the residues of past experiences come floating up before the consciousness in a stream in which there are frequent "forks in the road." The direction taken at a given time is effected by the easiest association of ideas, determined by the force of the old waking-state experience or by ease due to familiarity or habit.

The very technical term "vāsanās" here translated as "impressions," is often translated as "desires." The root of this word is vās, which means "to perfume," so it might be said that our stream of dreaming is just our perfume, or smell, or stink. It is not without significance that smell is perhaps the strongest of the senses in the effect of awakening memory-associations — very useful to animals. It is to be noted, too, that there is no difference between day-dreaming and dreaming-during-sleep. In both cases there is the absence of sensing of the outside world, in the one case by sleep of the senses, in the other by inattentiveness. Thus, being awake is nothing but the awakening of the senses. Other activities of the body — digestion, breathing, etc. — go on even when "we are asleep," which means when the senses are not in operation.

It may be asked: "Why is the word buddhi used in this connection?" Let us be very clear on this point. We are thinking of the inner instrument of consciousness, which gives us consciousness of self (ahankāra) and consciousness of ātman, the *real* Self. This is called chid-ātman. The conscious man or human consciousness, is, so to say, polluted or stained by awareness of things other than itself. More exactly, this means it is limited. To compare — suppose you were to take white light and color it red or green or any other color; you would then no longer see the *white* light. The principles of man are like the colors: — the ahankāra is consciousness of limited or defined or separate self, the buddhi is consciousness of other self (duality; "me" inside me, and the world "outside me").

The ahankāra has in some modern interpretations been called "the human ātman," or "the human monad," and the real ātman is then called "the divine ātman," (ātman and ātmā are the same word, of course, always). But in Chūd-āmani and all other Vedantic literature this is never done; the first three of the four constituents of the "inner instrument" are always given as ahankāra-buddhi-manas, never as ātma-buddhi-manas, and ātman is understood as beyond these, for which reason it is often called parātman (the ātman beyond), or paramātman (the supreme ātman).

It must be mentioned, however, that in popular Sanskrit literature, as distinguished from religious and philosophical literature (that is, in stories, poetry, etc.) we have ātman used as just "myself," any self. We have then such expressions as ātma-ja, meaning a son (literally "born of oneself"), also ātma-tyago (self-giving-up, which can be either self-sacrifice or suicide), also ātma-mana, which is pride. Also ātmiya commonly means "belonging to oneself" or "one's own."

It is, of course, to be understood that the "inner instrument" is always with us — there would be no conscious awareness *of* anything (except oneself) without the buddhi. So one cannot treat "the higher Self" as a sort of captive balloon, or speak of *"my* higher Self." All the principles of man have to be present, but some are more matured or developed than others. Also it is not good psychology to think of oneself as the lower self, as we are truly human only when thinking honestly and loving genuinely. To that we may add: and when being self-aware, as fully self-aware as we can be.

Verses 99 etc. will tell us more about the ātman.

CHAPTER 3

AWARENESS OF SELF

We have mentioned that there is consciousness of self (chidātman). This is what the Chūdāmani gives as ahan-kāra (the I-maker). This may be seen clearly if we observe the state of consciousness of a young baby. It knows only itself. It feels pleasure and pain, but does not ascribe these to anything outside itself. It does not know of anything outside itself.

Then at some point there dawns upon it "something out-side me" or "the world." This second stage is the rise of duality in consciousness. The name for this is buddhi, which equals "consciousness of," while ahankāra (the *human* monad, what the modern Theosophists call the human ātman) is merely consciousness. It is suggested that the reader now "look within" and, in a momentary act of medi-tation, perceive these two both present — the human self or consciousness (ahankāra or "ātman") and the intelligence or knowledge-of (buddhi).

At this point the babe's dawn of intelligence could be represented as an expression of astonishment: "Great Scott! There is a world outside me." And it stares in round-eyed wonder. Then comes a third experience or awakening, of the mental, which then begins to try to appraise things for the purpose of avoiding pain or of obtaining pleasure.

Coming now to our familiar states of consciousness, we have the (1) waking (jāgrat), in which we are aware that all sorts of things are bumping into us and poking into us, then (2) dream (swapna), in which the senses are asleep or not being attended to, and only memories of the bumpings and pokings are streaming along. Here we come to verse 99, which describes how one should avoid confusing this with the state of the Atman, and may learn to become *constantly aware of the true self-consciousness even in the midst of the waking state* and so no longer entirely victimized by them or in bondage to them. So:

99 (a). (The dream state) having set up (in itself) the forms of doer, etc. (the whole state of doing and experiencing) it manifests (before the consciousness).

99 (b). Where really only the Self Beyond (parāt-man) itself is shining; the mere conditioned (upādhi) intelligence is (now) the witness (consciousness), not being stained (interfered with) by pieces of "dones" and doings (things and actions).

99 (c). Because it is unattached (by desire) it is not stained by actions, by any limitation whatever, nor by "dones" (things, i.e. anything that has been made, produced or effected).

Comment. The fact of "attachment by desire" is very closely studied in this philosophy. We are free, but things get into us because we are interested in them, and we are interested because of desire, which includes both desire for the presence of the thing and desire against the presence of it (aversion).

100 (a). The subtle body is the instrument (or tool) in all the operations of the conscious self, the man.

100 (b). Like the chisels, etc. of a carpenter.

100 (c). That being so, this Self (ātman) is truly unattached.

101 (a). Blindness, dullness and sharpness are qualities (dharmas) only of the eye, arising only from the effect of its good or bad qualities. Similarly deafness, dumbness, etc. are (due to) qualities of the ear, etc.

101 (b). Not at all of the knower, the Self.

102 (a). The actions of inbreathing, outbreathing, yawning, sneezing, sweating, etc. are actions of the vitalities (prāna, etc.)—say those who understand them.

102 (b). Hunger and thirst are (however) the qualities (dharmas) of the vitality (prāna) itself.

Comment. A great distinction is to be noted between the operations by which various functions are carried on in the body, and the much more fundamental facts of hunger and thirst, which are promptings to the very provision of the body itself. (The reader may refer back to verse 95 for a list of the five main functions listed as prānic functions.)

103. The inner instrument (i.e., the mind) is in these eyes, etc. in the body. There it stands saying "I," by an assumption, by a reflection of the true light (tejas).

Comment. This is very significant. The first and only reality known in consciousness is itself — "I." Now, as the mind operates in its fourfold way (see verse 93) it makes the mistake of calling the mind "I." This is the fundamental error of ascription (adhyāsa), like that of a villager who mistakes a rope for a snake in the twilight. This is the primal error or piece of positive ignorance (avidyā) which leads to actions (form-making) which produce a foolish environment or world of things. (The whole question of illusion is to be taken up in verses 108 to 123). The wrong things also are mistaken for the right things, which leads to the whole business of running after things in pursuit of happiness which they cannot give.

104 (a). The I-maker (ahankāra) is what should be understood. It is the doer, the experiencer (of pleasure and pain) — this pretender (or presumer, or assumer).

104 (b). In conjunction with the qualities (gunas) of harmony (sattwa) etc. (i.e. sluggishness, restlessness, and well-adjusted orderliness) it experiences the three states (of waking, dreaming, and deep sleep).

105. It has pleasure when the sense-objects are agreeable, and misery in the reverse of that. Pleasure and pain (or happiness and misery) are *its* qualities (dharmas) — not of the always joyous ātman.

Comment. Here we touch the root of our common impulses, which is egotism. Everyone wants *to be,* not primarily *to do* or *to have,* we may say, "I want to own a fine house and garden." But look closely; it means, "I want *to be* the owner and enjoyer of a fine house and garden." There is a story of a little boy and ice-cream, and the dictum of the philosopher-onlooker: "That boy does not like ice-cream. He likes the consciousness of the taste of the ice-cream. If he could get that without the ice-cream he would be equally happy." It is all egoism or egotism.

106. An object is not in itself valuable. For the purpose of the Self only it is to be valued. Indeed, since of

all things the Self is inherently the most valuable, the Self is always joyous. Never is there sorrow (or misery) for this.

Comment. The word here translated "valuable" could just as accurately be translated "loved"; it contains both meanings.

107. Scripture, direct experience, tradition and reasoning (all) testify that in deep sleep, *without any object* (either factual or mental) the joy of the Self is experienced.

Comment. All the commentators on this topic point out that everybody really enjoys dreamless sleep, and add that on waking from it one exclaims with great pleasure: "Ah, I slept well." This statement is not considered to be a piece of reasoning: "Oh, I feel well now, so I must have slept well," but as a *memory* of the enjoyment of formless bliss actually experienced. It is not regarded as unconsciousness, but as unconsciousness-of.

Māyā: we come now to the topic māyā, often translated as "illusion" because the same word is used for common conjuring shows. The root of the word māyā means to "measure off," "mark off" or "mete out." It means essentially that things are both viewed and produced *limitedly* (not merely as to quantity, but as to quality, meaning, significance and utility) so that any one of them represents much more the absence of all other things than the presence of itself. This operation is a denial of the spiritual unity of all values or truth "beyond spaces and times" — or, more accurately, beyond separation.

108. There is a power of the Supreme Will which is called the Unmanifest. It is the Unknowing (avidyā) — which has no beginning. It has the nature of the three qualities (of inertia, energy and order). It is beyond

(everything). It is māyā, inferable from its effects by the greatly intelligent. By it all this world is begotten.

Comment. Every human endeavor to conceive the nature of the ultimate basis or source of the world has resulted only in describing an effect. But the cause must be different from the effect (notwithstanding the inviolability of natural law), for if they were not so they would be alike, the cause would be the same as the effect, and then there would be no cause and no effect.

In our common and familiar analysis of the world of our ordinary experience we find the mind acting as changer of forms (cause) and matter and motion as its effects. Legs do not walk on their own initiative. Iron does not seek the fire which melts it. So much is this the case that probably the best definitions of mind and matter are: matter is that which brings the past into the present; mind is that which brings the future into the present. Some say there can be no future in the present. Yet here it is, in the form of forethought. (Poor Prometheus chained to the rock.)

Now, in mind we have the familiar trio of will, feeling, and thought, and a little inspection reveals the supremacy of the first of these three, since the will is concerned with being, feeling with doing, and thought with having. It is then clear that the thought end of this trio is concerned with getting things and keeping them as long as you want. At the other end of the trio, the will is a mystery to the thought. Perhaps the nearest that we can get to it in thought is that it is perpetually concerned with more being, the enhancement of its living.

So we have found the reason for the expression "The Supreme Will" in our verse. The Prime Mover (Theos) means the prime willer, not primarily the prime thinker or planner, for indeed the old order changeth giving place to new, and no doings or havings are permanent, nor are they aiming at being permanent; nor are they aiming at even a temporary permanence, or in other words a sequence. There is no objective goal.

We have the word *Isha* in our verse. It is sometimes translated Ruler, Lord or God. The word *Ichchhā* means Will, and there is nothing to be ruled until the world is formed. Thus in our human minds we govern our acts by our thoughts and feelings, and we govern our thoughts and feelings by our will, which has its own secret purpose, if such it can be called.

Then comes the power (shakti). It is seen in the process of "one thing at a time," not all at once, — *i.e.,* operation ignorance, or ignoring, or unknowing. This is the same as veiling, which means partially hiding. The veiled face looks different from the unveiled. The thinking mind — so obviously concerned with the moment that its first act is always concentration on some topic (an act of time, of unknowing) — works with the veiled. It cannot look upon the unveiled and continue to be itself.

The action of the body (operation space) follows the thought in the mind, when the thought is poised by the will. Thoughts are ruled by the will; body-actions by the thought. (As shown in the well-known fact that most people cannot walk on a plank say fifty feet up in the air without falling. They fall because they *think* of falling. To do it without falling, the will must change the mental picture. The squirrels and birds have no trouble in this respect.)

I need barely mention the pains of time and the pains of space, how fundamental they are — supreme pointers to supreme freedom, or union with the will, beyond the ahankāric or egoistic error, never the same for two successive moments.

In verse 109 it is stated that Māyā cannot be described in terms of any categories whatever. On the contrary, it can be spoken of only as a perfectly wonderful power, perfectly indescribable. Yet, we may add, it is logically necessary for the existence of a world in which all facts and values are limited and relative. Verse 110 states that all such relative realities are illusory, and can be terminated only by realization of the pure Brahman, one only, or rather "without a second."

The following is a condensed summary of verses 111 to 123 which describe the effects of the three aspects of māyāvic operation known as the tāmasic, rājasic and sāttwic (inertia, energy, and law). The rājasic operation is called vikshepa, which means "throwing out." This agrees with the theory of "objective ideation." In this view all things are really existential, and can exist and operate apart from the mind that formed them. In the mind rajas is seen in the emotions that promote action. The tāmasic operation is called āvriti or āvarana, which veils or hides the full truth about anything, leading the rajas to build with "partials" and so produce an actual world of illusion. To take this world at its face value is to see and act with ignorance.

But sattwa sees into the essentials of things, and as such is the intelligent function of the mind, guiding its acts into paths of law and order even when it has an admixture of rajas and tamas.

When the sattwa is pure the mind catches a clear view of the non-relative Self, and thus achieves tranquillity, poise and happiness, which then replaces the old hunting and acquiring instincts of tamas and rajas which lead to the continuity and increase of life in the world. But when the sattwa is mixed with tamas and rajas there is no longer personal pride, but the practice of virtues (the five — cleanliness, contentment,

self-mastery, study and attentiveness to the Supreme Will),
and of restraints (from injuring, lying, theft, sensuality and
greed), also confidence in the Law and in oneself, dedication,
eagerness for liberation from the bondage of this world, also
the divine achievements (control of mind and body, freedom
from superstition, fortitude, confidence and steadiness) and
turning away from the unreal motives and interests. As the
vision of the Self becomes pure, all the world, right up to
māyā itself, is seen to be the not-Self.

CHAPTER 4

NATURE OF THE SUPREME SELF

The teacher, changing the subject, proceeds:

124. Now I will describe fully to you the self-nature of the Supreme Self, having discerned which a man is released from bondage, and experiences independence (kaivalya).

Comment. Sometimes the term moksha (liberation) is used, sometimes kaivalya (independence). The latter was used by Patañjali, in his *Yoga-Sūtras,* for the goal of yoga-effort.

125. There is some sort of eternal Self (swayam) which is the foundation of the notion of "I," is the see-er of the three states (of waking, dreaming and deep sleep), and is of different character from the five coverings (koshas).

Comment. The five sheaths, coverings or bodies are described as composed of (a) food. (b) vitality, (c) mentality, (d) valuation or discernment and (e) joyous life.

126. This "I" knows all about buddhi and its productions (or activities), as to their presence and their absence in the (three states of) waking, dreaming and sleeping.

Comment. What in modern thought are called the objective and the subjective are respectively the objects and notions in the world (bodily life) and the mind (mental life). The sleeping state is beyond these, there being in that state neither objects nor thoughts of them but only the consciousness without them.

127. This "I" itself sees everything (when seen), but nothing sees it. It (alone) gives perceptiveness to buddhi etc., and is not provided with perceptivity by them.

128. It is That by which all this universe is pervaded. Nothing pervades it. All this (universe) is its shining (manifestation), for it reflects (only) when shone upon.

129. By the mere proximity (or presence) of This, the body, the senses, the mind and (even) the buddhi move in their own proper departments, life messengers.

130. By This, which has the very nature of constant knowing, are known (all the constituents of man) beginning at ahankāra (the I-maker) and ending at the body, also objects, and pleasure, etc. (feelings) — just as (for example) a jar.

Comment. The constituents or principles of man, taken in order, are, ahankāra, buddhi, manas (mind), prāna (vitality) and deha (body). The higher principles widely popularized in the West by H. P. Blavatsky from the same source and given as ātman, buddhi and manas, do not really differ from these, because the ātman there given is specifically stated to be only "the human ātman," not the divine ātman, which is beyond. It is then also spoken of as "an undetached spark." A philosophical understanding of this arises when it is observed that the divine ātman is not divided up, is non-dual, is in fact the One. The human ātman, or ahankāra, is then the principle which reflects (or receives in itself, like a mirror, this one-ness) and then applies it (i.e., the one-ness) to itself, making itself into an individual entity, *a one,* and then, through buddhi, seeing others (others like me), fellow-sparks, so to say, and through manas individual objects — which last are, of course, only temporarily seen, or provisionally regarded, as individual facts, for they are really always undergoing change.

I may mention incidentally that meditation on the true nature of others in the light of these facts is *most* revealing and rewarding. It puts a new face on our human relations.

131. This is the inside Self, the ancient dweller in the organism (purusha), the experiencer of uninterrupted complete happiness, who is always of the same nature, awareness as such. Impelled by That, speech and the vital airs act.

132. Here indeed, in the pure mind, in the depths of buddhi, in the unmanifest ether (ākāsha), is the dawnlight. Like the sun high in the sky it shines by its own light, lighting all this world.

Comment. Here one is instructed not to look for the Self outside, but here in this very body, mind, higher intelligence and essential supersensible nature.

133. The Knower, amidst the changes in mind and egoism (i.e., self-image), and the changes made by the body, the senses and the vitality, (although) following those like fire in iron, does not act (upon them) nor is changed at all.

Comment. It is, of course, easy to observe by simple introspection that one's thoughts and feelings are quite *objective* to the self which observes them, and that this observer is not at all of the character of those thoughts and feelings, which change in themselves and also produce or effect change in the world. But just as a ball of red-hot iron seems to be a ball of fire, so does the Self seem *from the outside* to have the form of what it observes.

134. It is not born, nor does it die. It does not grow or decay, nor change form ever. Even in the dissolution of this body this Self is not dissolved — like the atmosphere in a pot.

Comment. When an earthen pot is destroyed the air which was in it is still there.

135. It is different from matter (prakriti) and its forms (vikritis). Its own being is pure knowing. Without being like them it illumines all this real and unreal (world) entirely. This Supreme Self (paramātman) flashes upon the waking and other states. By its (very) nature of being it declares, "I am I."

Comment. One is reminded of the statement of Jehovah (Exodus, 3, 14): "I am that *I* am." This was evidently a warning, to ward off anthropomorphism, but seemingly has not been so understood. Otherwise, there would have been no sense or purpose in such a statement.

Now follows the teacher's advice:

136. Know thou this government of the mind (manas), saying "I am this myself Self in this self," through the witnessing, and through the purity of buddhi. Cross the present ocean of running about (sansara) with its wave of births and deaths. Be one who has accomplished his purpose (kritartha). Stand firm in the nature of Brahman (God).

We shall come now to a series of verses explaining how men are caught in the bondage of material life.

CHAPTER 5

CAUSES OF TROUBLES OR BONDAGES

The group of verses to which we have now come deals with the two causes of the present condition of men. The statement is that men are in their present state of bondage, or dependence, as a result of these two causes, and the pity is that they go on and on, operating the same two continuously and thereby involving themselves again and again in a struggle to avoid pain. It is not held that these men have created positive pain as such, but it is maintained that they have manufactured all their painful conditions, and put themselves into those conditions.

The trouble began when the amoeba began to organize itself. It said to itself — so to speak — "Let me have a mouth for eating and legs for propelling myself along, and then I shall not have the trouble of making these each time I want to eat or to swim or walk. Then all that I will need to do when I want to eat or walk will be to tell those appendages to go to work." What he did not bargain for was that he would have to carry those machines about with him and protect them against their own special dangers. A modern man does not carry his motor-car with him on his back, so as to have it available when he wants to go for a run in it, but he has to provide a home — a place of safety for it, and do something about that. And so on and on. First feet, then shoes for the feet, then a closet for the shoes, then . . . and so on. Such is *the world*.

As soon as this organization begins there are possessions and when there are possessions there is bondage. Every organ is a limitation, legs are not wings, and the motor-car cannot act as an airplane. "But," says the man (if he is not wealthy), "I can use the public airplane." So also the bus, and let the car go. "But with the car I can go where I want, and when I want." And so on . . .

The two continuing *causes of bondage* are stated in these verses as: (1) Veiling, (āvarana), and (2) Projection (vikshepa).

> *Verse 137.* The idea, "Here I am in the not-self," is bondage for a man. It has arisen through ignorance. It is the cause of his meeting with the troubles of birth and death. Only because of this, with his understanding (buddhi) of self, he says that this unreal body is the real. He nourishes it, cleans it and protects it with various sense-objects, (and so is bound) as a silkworm by its threads.

Comment. We have to study man as he now finds himself, in the midst of a vast number and variety of created forms in the world. Not only manufactured objects, designed and planned by the mind, are products or projections of that mind, but even his body and the bodies of various plants and animals are indirectly projections (vikshepas) resulting from their desires. As Jennings puts it — the seal did not take to the water because it had flippers, but it grew flippers because it took to the water. Similarly, all the objects that man has made are the result of his thoughts or actions. They are all vikshepas.

Those vikshepas are all based upon veilings. If a human being is born as a female, her masculine tendencies of thought, action and feeling are discouraged or set aside (veiled) by her parents and by herself. The feminine virtues and tendencies are discouraged and set aside in the case of a boy. This veiling applies to everything. People have biased opinions on everything, and the bias in every case is the outcome of a previous bias.

Allied to the doctrine of āvarana (veiling) is the teaching about absence (technically called abhāva). If there is the presence of something, there is the absence of something else, so every action involves particular attention and therefore the *absence* of something else; every thought of a thing involves the absence or exclusion (veiling) of something else. We say, "This is a horse, not a cow." Old logicians of India would have worded it, "There is an absence of cow in the horse." Everything excludes everything else. The more you are a woman the less you are a man, and vice versa.

This again leads to another doctrine — that of ascription or assumption (adhyāsa). This means that every time you look at or think of something, some prior thought will come up out of your mind — from past experience or thought (i.e. by habit) — and bias or even pervert your present view, mental, emotional, and even sensuous. This is veiling again, in another form.

So — to be brief — in the thought of "what I am" there is generally a veiling. A false "self" is set up, and then the acts of that self will be chosen and performed on the basis of that wrong judgment. Productions and associations will be based on this veiling and projecting, leading to more and more absence of the *real self* and its *real happiness*.

It is to be noted in this matter that *existence implies non-being*. What then are you? Something not of the nature of *anything* in your field of existence, since all that is known within that field veils that reality. But we must take up this matter after studying the following group of verses:

Verse 138. His idea of what *is not* the fact arises in the deluded person because of darkness (ignorance). It is clearly on account of absence of discernment that it jumps up — like the thought of a rope with regard to a snake. Thus a very great assemblage of valueless (things and thoughts) descends upon the one who accepts (the wrong understanding). Thus he who holds to the false becomes bound indeed. Give heed, O friend!

Comment. The little story of the rope and the snake is a common illustration of the effect of ignorance (avidyā or ajñāna). The story goes that a man, coming along, steps on the snake, thinking it to be only a piece of rope, with dire consequences.

Verse 139. The infinitely splendid Self *is* (however) being expressed, by the power of the knowledge of what is unbroken (non-relative), eternal and unitary (advaya). The veiling power, however, which is made of darkness (ignorance) covers it up — as the eclipse does the disc of the sun.

Comment. In the old folk-lore, Rāhu was a demon who was supposed to swallow the sun and moon for a while periodically, and even now some village people may be seen and heard beating drums and making other noises to frighten the demon away while the eclipse is on. In Indian astrology Rāhu is one of the planets.

Verse 140. When there is this distortion of the perfectly stainless and brilliant own-self, the man, through (his) delusion, regards the not-self-body as "I." Then the great power of rajas (energy and emotion) which is called vikshepa (projection) afflicts him by the binding qualities of desire, anger, etc.

Comment. A common assumption, not mentioned here, is that life is for enjoyment. The two causes of creation or production, however, indicate that it is for the *education* of the "liv-er." When *things* are pursued, with the wrong idea in mind, there comes only bondage. People surround themselves with things as a result of (1) the wrong valuation, and (2) the projection and production on that basis. But if the direct value of work *to the doer* is the motive, the benefit of the *doing* is found. The object of human life is to cultivate the human being — growth through exercise — and then in the maturing of one "faculty" there is a seed-bed, so to say, for the next. Thus emotion corrects laziness, mentality corrects emotion, love (ethic) corrects mentality, and spirituality, when it comes, corrects love. The correction, in every case, removes some kind of pain, and at the same time ensures the exercise and growth of the "sprouting" higher principle. The higher principle then directs and *uses* the lower impulse, instead of *serving* it. Moral laws or formulas by man are primarily due to mental selection and guidance of emotions for personal and social health, and later (when voluntary) become ethical as well. Avarana (veiling) and vikshepa (projection) are two highly technical words in this philosophy. When they have operated there stands up the environment in front of you. *Doing* has been replaced by *having,* and having then involves much bondage unless the having is for the higher aim, directly or indirectly and — best of all — consciously so.

Verse 141. The (pure) intelligence which is the (direct) perceiver of the Self is eclipsed by the devouring crocodile (or shark), the Great Delusion. Then, by the quality of that, he (the man) imagines himself to be in the various conditioned states. Sinking and rising in the shoreless ocean of embodied existence (sansāra), he wanders about. Horrible thought! Damnable occurrence!

Verse 142. Just as a group of clouds produced by the rays of the sun rises up, obscuring the sun — so the Ego (ahankāra), produced by the Self, having hidden the essential nature of the Self, manifests itself.

Verse 143. Just as on a bad day, when the lord of day (the sun) is overcome by dense clouds, and fierce cold, rain and wind afflict them, so also when the Self is covered up by unbroken darkness, the poignant vikshepa-power (projection) dominates the deluded intelligence (buddhi) with great miseries.

Verse 144. From these two powers, indeed, the bondage of man has come to be. Deluded by these two he wanders about, regarding the body as the Self.

Comment. This is the end of the series of verses describing avarana and vikshepa (veiling and projecting). We now come to four verses which speak of the nature of the bondage and the means of its cessation.

Verse 145. Of the tree of embodied existence, —

    (a) darkness (ignorance) is the seed,

    (b) the idea that the body is the Self is the sprout,

    (c) desire is the leafing,

    (d) action is the sap,

    (e) the body is the trunk,

    (f)   vitality is the branch-maker,

    (g) the senses are its tips (or points),

    (h) the sense-objects are the flowers,

    (i)   troubles (including pain) are the fruit,

    (j)   the experiencer, the life (jīva) is the bird.

Comment. Here the entire world is regarded as a tree. Every form in the world, whether natural or artificial (those of growth or those made by actions of body and mind), is produced by the positive action (vikshepa) of jīvas (lives), such action being based upon erroneous suppositions. These natural and artificial forms then react on the life, on the principle that what you make you have until you unmake it (called the law of karma).

Verse 146. The root-ignorance, the bondage of the not-Self (anātman) is innate (or inherent), without beginning and without end — it is declared. It produces the baleful stream of miseries in birth, death, illness and decrepitude.

Verse 147. It is not possible to break (this bondage) by missile weapons nor by hand weapons (or tools), not by wind, nor by fire, nor by ten million actions (of any kind) — without the great sword of discerning (viveka) knowledge and the lovely bright grace of the Upholder (Dhātri).

Comment. Some may translate the word Dhātri (literally, Upholder) as God, and I do not think Shankara, if he were here, would object. He might question, however, what was meant by the word God. Whatever That is from which all powers of ours (whether material, mental, or moral) are subtractions (by avidyā) and all productions of ours are fancies (in some degree like "Alice in Wonderland" or "A Midsummer Night's Dream"), the basic power of being (both being and the maker of being ‚as such) has to be greater than all — greater in whatever greatness they may have, and greater with a non-relative greatness that our thought and love do not know. The Dhātri has to be "without shadow of turning." All is from That, and of its grace, pregnant with the ideals of perfect intelligence and love. It is the *Absolute Presence,* the apotheosis of God. There is one thing that is not relative but is absolute in this world of ours and that is unity, which makes intellect to be intelligent and makes the world to be intelligible, and makes love to be loving. Subtractions from it, but still heralds and harbingers of its nature are the individuality (or unity) in the varieties, and harmony in the lives of lives. Variety still requires the ever-present unity, since each is a one.

It is in this admission of God that Shankara's doctrine is different from that of Buddha, as passed on to us by the Elders, but even so Buddha disapproved of negative statements about Nirvāna as much as he did of positive ones.

"Grace," then, is also not an unsuitable word in this verse. To receive grace is then much the same thing as to give up error, which is impurity, in either thought or love. It is the acceptance of unity, which is in some degree lacking in the very nature of our thought and our love. It is the acceptance of life which is of the nature of *being,* beyond *havings,* beyond *doings,* beyond even the doings of the mind. If That has any doing, it is the doing-of-being, but of course we must admit that the doing of being is really no doing but being. And as to grace: it *is* a grace, is it not, and not a doing, that the pains of the body (especially hunger) give birth to positive desire (e-motion), that the pains of emotion are reduced by the intellect, that the pains (frustrations and boredoms) of the intellect are relieved by the coming of love, and the pains of love will be relieved by the arrival of spiritual experience, with its new message of unity.

> *Verse 148.* Faith in one's own rightness (dharma) rising from a definite opinion (without uncertainty) as to the correctness of the "heard" (shruti) (i.e. the Veda or declaration — scripture) — by exactly that there is purification of the self (ātman) of this (man). From the

purified understanding (buddhi) there is perception of the Supreme Self. Only by that is there the de-struction of the embodied existence (sansāra), with its root (the ignorance).

Comment. It comes as a surprise to some that "faith" should come in here, where they expect reason above all. It does, however, naturally accompany the idea of grace. If we are to be responsive to the behests of some impulse or idea not received by either the senses or reason, there must be some receptiveness. There must then be a response (or obedience of the nature of a choice) in the mind, and in action and feeling. It must not be *against* reason, when that is concerned with welfare, of oneself or others. And yet this faith must have a region of origin and a state to which it calls us, which is beyond welfare, though it is a new and better welfare, and is known to be such when it becomes known. Reason is under law, and is useful — or indeed usable — only under that.

This "faith" is related to duty (dharma) or what one *ought* to do, to feel or to think about. This duty is called dharma. It is "the right"; anything against it is wrong. The word dharma comes from the root "dhri," to uphold or maintain. The word "Dhātri," which we have translated "Up-holder," has exactly the same root. All that is offered to us, or rather presented for our acceptance or reception by that Upholder, is a grace — something not made by ourselves as we know ourselves, but a gift, a present.

So, then, when a man does his duty, acts according to his duty, he is *obeying* this faith, and his duty is clearly what-he-can-do. In doing what he can he is upholding his portion of the world, and also is maintaining his own abilities (bodily, mentally, and morally or ethically). The law with reference to this is easily seen — by the use of thought, thought grows; by the use of love, love grows. We must add to that: "By the use of the spirit, the spirit grows." When thought and love have reached their maturity and it becomes evident that they cannot go on getting bigger and bigger forever (just as arms and legs cannot) also that *their* pains must be solved by something else, superior to them, they become the seed-bed for spiritual "knowledge," spiritual experience, spiritual operation, and spiritual growth.

How spirit is concerned with the ātman (real Self) and the ahankāra (ego), can well be explained in connection with the next group of verses.

CHAPTER 6

DISCRIMINATION BETWEEN SELF AND SELF

Having in the last group of verses discussed the reason for man's bondage to circumstances, and having learned about the day in which these limitations were produced by him himself, we turn now to examine his bodies — those productions most intimate to him — to which he is bound by strong desires. The mere fact, however, that he feels the bondage is irksome and resents it, indicates that the free Self is not *entirely* immersed.

The Sanskrit word for bodies which is used in these verses is "kosha." Literally, it means a covering or envelope, and is also used for such things as the scabbard of a sword. (The sh in kosha is very soft.)

Verse 149. Covered by the five vestures (koshas) — that made by food (the material body) and the others — produced by his innate power, the Self does not shine forth. It is (obscured) like the water standing in a pond having coatings of algae.

Verse 150. When the covering of algae is removed the perfectly pure water is obtained. It allays the affliction of thirst, immediately giving great happiness to the man.

Comment. In the following verses the five vestures will be listed in order, as:
(1) The vesture made of food (anna-māyā-kosha).
(2) That made of vital breath (prāna-māyā-kosha).

(3) That made of thought and feeling (mano-māyā-kosha).

(4) That made of understanding (vijñāna-māyā-kosha).

(5) That made of joy (ānanda-māyā-kosha).

No mention is made as to *how* the Self produces these bodies, but with advancement in knowledge we nowadays distinguish between production-by-desire and production-by-plan. A glove is produced by planned thought and action in a certain environment, that is, *intelligent response* to cold. But the hand was produced by *desire* of a creature wanting to get about in trees; gradually, in the course of generations, by the elimination of unfit variations, it became more qualified to do so. Without the desire in either case — the planning affecting the environment and producing an artifact, or the desiring necessary for a natural modification of the body (without thought) — no production, either of glove or hand, would have occurred.

It is the coming-in of the mental predominance in the human stage of development which has so enormously substituted artifacts for adaptations. Man has adapted the environment to himself (and not himself to the environment) to such an extent that he has now no fur or feathers, but only manufactured clothing. We wonder what the new "air-conditioning" will lead to in the course of a long time; shall we some day have a race of human beings who have lost all adaptiveness to varying temperatures, and must live from birth to death inside "air-conditioned" boxes, or suits or machines?

It is understandable that the belief in this self-production of the bodies could spread among the Hindu Aryans on account of their view that life is reincarnating. While the West has held to the perpetuity of *the same matter,* the East has preferred the idea of *the same life.* Their old folk-lore shows (in the Purānas) past ages — the fish age, the animal age, etc. in story form.

Evolution has to do with *forms,* of course, in which we see life and matter mingling. We see that it is the life-principle that promotes new forms and the matter-principle that holds them firm and steady. We see also that the life-principle thus represents the future and the matter-principle the past, so much so that the best definition of matter now appears to be: "That which carries the past into the present." On the other hand, the life, with its innate discontent, or rather dissatisfaction with what is, shows itself in a desire for "more life," and thus appears to be the funnel for a "potential" which leads to more and more form-building, together with an organizing unity ("inherent coherence" in evolutionary terms) which makes it the builder or producer of both bodies and artifacts. In this way it is the future that dominates the past in the world of our senses. So the view that the Self is responsible for the production of its own bodies is not inconsistent with modern knowledge and thought.

The author of the Chūdāmani now proceeds with two assertions: (1) that man can know his very Self, and (2) that this may be done by not letting his mind be governed by his body.

> *Verse 151.* On the rejection (mentally) of the five vestures (or bodies) the pure (self) shines forth, the undiluted essence of eternal joy, the original (or true) being, supreme and self-luminous (in all respects).

> *Verse 152.* Discrimination between (what is) Self (āt-man) and (what is) not-Self should be done by the wise person, for the sake of release from bondage. Only by that does he become happy, having known himself as

being (sat), and consciousness (chit) and joy (ānanda).
Verse 153. Having discriminated the original unattached
and unproduced Self from the classes of seen things —
like the reed (withdrawn) from a rush — he who is free
(or liberated) stands (or remains) with that Self, having countered (or negatived) everything there.

We now come to a group of verses (154 to 164) which
give reasons why a man should not mistake his body for
himself. To save space I will briefly list the items mentioned
in these verses. The body lives on food and dies if it does not
obtain it; it is composed of skin, bones, flesh, etc.; it is very
temporary — does not exist before birth or after death; it is
a mere sense-object; it has various limbs, without some of
which it can carry on; it has changes, which are not of the
same nature as the conscious Self which observes the changes
and abides from first to last. One must look meditatively at
the body, comparing each item with that which looks at the
item (oneself), summing up "How could this thing possibly
be myself?" so as to obtain a clear, strong and constant idea.
Mere book-learning or theory will not produce the desired
effect, which will become the background feeling or thought
on all occasions — that one is the Self, not subject to the listed
limitations, but eternal (out of time) and free. Just, it concludes, as you do not imagine that your shadow is yourself,
or your body pictured in dreams, or yourself as objective in
imagination, so also realize that the body is not yourself.
Thus destroy this error — which is only mental — which produces desires which lead to actions, which lead to rebirth.

Comment. One can see that in this matter there is ignorance (here mental) at work, with its two effects — veiling and
projection — resulting in material productions which, being
material, are self-continuing until counteracted. We may take

into account also that in this philosophy, desires (kāma) for things (possessions or havings) also come into the category of mental thoughts (manas). Life is not for the pleasure of *having* (or sense-pleasures); these sense-pleasures were only intended to stimulate the undeveloped mind into working for the welfare of the body (eating, when hungry, etc.), as may be observed in the lives of most wild animals, and when the human mind works to get pleasures beyond this (elaborate spiced, salted and sugared foods to stimulate the jaded appetite, spiced literature and pictures intended to excite excessive sex-activity for pleasure, etc.) there is kāma (desire). The *Bhagavad-Gītā* makes it clear, however, that kāmas which are in the line of duty or law are good (Ch. 6, 11). They are valuable, because the body is valuable as a jumping-off place for the mind, like the ground and the foot.

We come next, in verse 165, to a statement about the vesture or body of "breath" (prāna), composed of the "vital airs" which guide the essential functions of the material body.

> *Verse 165.* The vital breath (prāna), influenced by the five action-organs becomes the vesture-made-of-vitality (prāna-māyā-kosha), filled with which this food-made (body or vesture), having the Self (within it), proceeds to function in all its actions.

Comment. This means that if this "vitality" were not within it the dense body would be unresponsive, inactive, dead, but when it is present the body takes on the direction of the life-functions (breathing, digestion, etc.) which furnish the action-organs (hands, feet, mouth, etc.) with their energy. There is a distinction between the body-functions which are mainly involuntary and go on with their work even during sleep, and those which are mainly responsive to thought, feeling and decision. It is said here that even the voluntary actions of the limbs could not take place without the mediation of this "vitality." We do in fact find that between the thought and the action there is the mediation of some sort of "electric" current, responsible for the unity (or coherence) of the body.

Verse 166. Even the prāna-māyā (vesture) is not the Self. It is (something) formed from wind (or air, vāyu), and like air it comes and goes in and out. Wherefore it never knows anything of what is pleasant or painful, of its own or of others, being always directed by something else.

Now we come to the third vesture or covering (kosha), the mental.

Verse 167. The organs of knowledge (or senses) and the mind (manas, from the root "man," to think) constitute the vesture-made-of-mind (mano-māyā-kosha), which is the cause of the distinguishing of things, including "I" and "mine." It is strong, holding in its grasp the several kinds of awareness. Having permeated the previous vesture (the prānic) it blossoms (into its activity).

Verse 168. The vesture-made-of-mind (mano-māyā-kosha) fire, blazing with the fuel of many desires, burns up the diversity (the world) by means of the five senses — the objects (of the world) being like a stream of melted butter being poured (into the sacrificial fire on the altar) by five sacrificial priests.

Verse 169. There is no ignorance (or error, avidyā) greater than that of the mind (manas), for the mind is the ignorance which is the cause of the bondage of material existence. When it is destroyed everything is destroyed; in its increase everything increases.

Comment. Those who have studied the principle of ignorance will remember that it begins with a limitation and then acts or creates on that basis. It is easy to see that the mind begins a thought by focusing upon a limited (or relative) object or idea, and then proceeds to expatiate from that angle or platform or point of view. Proceeding still further to action, it then creates more and more things.

Thought is especially concerned with material things, because these are fixed and predictable. It can deal with ideas also, but only if these are fixed or defined. When objects or ideas are called up in the mind for purposes of comparison as to similarities and differences or for classification, the images must be faithful unchanging replicas of fact — water must be water, fire fire, and earth earth. Mental thinking cannot be done with reference to other living beings, except as they have expressed themselves in body or other habits — a habit of mind having something of the character and fixity of material things. Otherwise they are too unpredictable.

Hence it can be seen that manas (the thinking mind) is specially concerned with the material world, and with the creation and alteration and use of forms therein. Its *doing* is concerned with *having,* even to the having of feelings and ideas, which become satisfactory to the mind insomuch as they are possessed by habit or available to memory. The mental process begins with *recognition* (an animal recognizes a thing seen before when it sees that thing again) and later on the mind advances to memory (or recall *in* the mind) and then, still later, to thought.

The mind is specially related to the five senses. It is sometimes called the sixth sense because it senses the senses (so to speak) and combines their very different messages in the thought of one object as, for example, the weight *and* hardness of iron (from touch), a distinction presented by two different senses — sight and touch.

Verse 170. In dream the mind creates according to its own power, in a void as regards object — a whole world, including the enjoyer (fancied self) and other things. It is (really) not different also in the waking state; all that (world) too is an expression (or projection) of this mind.

Verse 171. When the mind is dissolved in deep sleep, there is nothing at all, as is well known. Therefore the mind-produced round of events (sansāra) is of no validity (or reality) for this man.

Comment. It is not suggested that the round of events (sansāra) is valueless, however. It has the same value as a doll has to a little girl, it is an aid to concentration. So is a piano to a musical composer. Concentration is followed by expansion without loss of the intensity of consciousness acquired in the concentration. And that is followed by unitary grasp, fullness without exclusion. Life in sansāra is thus, "One thing at a time, and that done well," the inner *effect* of which is never lost. In deep sleep, the Vedānta declares, there is not unconsciousness, but a total cessation of the mental process of spreading things out. It is the happy state, without the bondage of limitation (veiling or āvarana) or the projection (vikshepa) of limitations into material fixity or continuity.

Verse 172. A cloud is brought by the wind and again by that it is taken away. Bondage is produced by the mind; liberation is also produced by that.

Verse 173. Having produced desire for the body and all objects, it binds the man by that as an animal in a net. Afterwards that very mind (manas) releases him from bondage, brought about by disgust, as if to poisons.

Comment. It is indeed well known to all that the sight of certain things or even the thought of them produces desire, and the satisfaction of the desire is not permanent. It is on account of this fact that no one has even been able to think of a satisfactory permanent heaven-life. Behind it all, of course, is the deeper desire (which will be spoken of in later verses) for "more life" and "better life," by some central impulse which never fails, carrying the man along through bodily pleasures to emotional pleasures and on to mental pleasures, and on to love and egoic pleasure, and even, upon maturity, to what we can only call spiritual pleasure.

Verse 174. Therefore he himself (through his mind) is the cause in the production of bondage *or* liberation (as the case may be) — the cause of bondage when stained by the qualities of eagerness (rajas), of liberation when pure, without eagerness (sattwa) or sluggishness (tamas).

Verse 175. Having attained purity through a pre-eminence of the qualities of discernment (or discrimination — viveka) and uncoloredness (or dispassion — vairāgya), the mind (manas) operates for liberation. Therefore by the wise, desiring liberation, these two are to be strengthened in the very beginning.

CHAPTER 7

THE USE OF THE MIND

The last two verses declared that the thinking mind is the cause of both bondage and liberation — bondage when tainted with the rajas quality (restless desire) and liberation when it has its own true sattwa quality (harmonious judgment). Harmonious living is first of all what is naturally beneficial to the body (not too much nor too little of food, exercise, and rest) and what is beneficial to the mind in all matters of imagination, investigation, study, and thought. Discriminatory judgment is to be used in all these matters. After stating in verse 176 that the mind (manas) can be a veritable "tiger in the jungle of sense-pleasures" if not used with discrimination of true values, and self-control as regards emotions, our author continues:

Verse 177. The mind (manas) constantly produces for the enjoyer sense-objects without end, by nature dense or subtle, and differing according to kind of body, social status, stage of life and outward circumstances, with their qualities, activities, causation and effects.

Verse 178. Having deluded the consciousness, which is (really) unattached (to things), and having enslaved it by the material qualities of body, senses and vitality, the mind (manas) causes it to wander about ceaselessly among experiences of fruits (results) brought about by its own actions.

Comment. Men's lives depend very much upon their ideas and opinions about things. Their actions arise from their states of mind, and in turn these actions produce their "karmas" in two ways: (1) in the form of what they are now making, and (2) as results of their past actions. In these two ways, operating in different proportions at different times, the entire contents of a person's "world" are produced. It is probable that the average man in India regards his condition of body, social status, etc., as due to his own actions (toward self and toward others) in past lives, while now, given those conditions, most of his daily experience results from the way in which he deals with them or makes use of them. Then, anything sufficiently unusual or uncalculated will be regarded by him as some particular irruption breaking into the present from the past. Such an uncalculated irruption he will call a piece of karma, not in the same class as the regular business of daily life.

Only thoughtful discrimination will show him that these things have no value in themselves, as the manas seems to indicate, but are valuable only for the inward growth that can be obtained from dealing with them (as a little girl develops her own potential by playing with a doll) — gains of strength and capacity which are carried on into future lives, while the "toys" fall away. When someone says "You cannot take it with you," he refers to the objects, not to the unfoldment of "more essential being" which you do "take with you." So, to speak in practical terms, a person can decide what he will have in future lives — material things, beauty, health, mental ability, more love nature, more will-power — then work at those things now, and so he will win more capacity in his own being, and will win those things for which he has worked. Be then cautious, says our author, and do not be deceived by appearances, but consider what is really worth while and then go for that. No failure can daunt the man who understands, for he knows that he gains by the trying, not the getting, and no failure can lessen that, while easy success can often reduce the effort and the further gain. Beware, then, it can be said, rather of success than of failure. As to the occasional (frequent or infrequent) blows from "past karma" — here too is the opportunity to "advance on stepping-stones of our dead selves."

> *Verse 179.* The repeated rebirth of the soul (purusha) is due to the fault of "wrong supposition" (adyāsa). By that (mind) this wrong-supposition-bondage is surely formed. This is the cause of the miseries of birth, etc., of the undiscerning . . . who has the faults of rajas and tamas.

> *Verse 180.* For this reason the learned men who have seen the truth have said that the mind *is* ignorance, by which all the people are moved about like clusters of clouds.

> *Verse 181.* Purification of one's mind (from these two tendencies) should be diligently done by one desiring liberation (from ignorance and its results). When this purity exists, liberation is as a fruit lying on the flat of the hand.

> *Verse 182.* Whoever, by intentness upon release and with faith in the truth, has renounced desire for things — all karmas — to the very root, and becomes devoted to reading and meditating — he shrugs off the rajasic nature from his higher intelligence.

Comment. Wrong supposition, mentioned in Verse 179, is a very important psychological term. It is defined as "the ascription of something previously seen to what is now seen." The classical example of this is the case of the villager coming home along the field-paths in the dusk of the evening. He jumps with alarm as he sees a snake in his way — but closer inspection shows it to be only a piece of rope. This snake-in-a-rope gives an example of fear, but what we are now considering is the reverse of this. People are seeing allurements — desirable things — in what are really not so. So far from increasing the happiness of life they positively diminish it by their cloying, clogging, stifling, suffocating stickiness. Where is the wrong ascription in this? They are mistaken for life. It is living that is of value, not having. It is living that is joyful, not possessions, not karmas. What you *do* is living; what you *have* is bondage. To be conscious of the "living" rather than holding on to things by letting them delude you into the false belief that they can "give" you pleasure or "bring" you anything is the correct change to make.

The reverse error — equally bad — is to reject things. To think that you can get rid of the bondage by casting off the things is again to imagine that things bind you. Turn your eye upon the living. No matter what the circumstances you can live — will, love, think, rejoice in the being of life. We are born to live as life. This is the first thing we know — this life — and it we know essentially as our very being. The fountain of life is in us, or rather is what we are, and it is joy. To imagine the joy-giver as outside us is the mistake. Correct the mental error and the rest will be easy.

The last word in verse 182 — higher intelligence (buddhi) — is significant. The error of the manas invades even the higher judgment. It too is tainted. Fight not, then, against wrong ideas, but seek pure judgment. Then the sky will clear and manas will be a shining tool in its operation of gaining knowledge about the relative characteristics of things. What you do with them will then depend on judgment (buddhi) or valuation, with the welfare of life (living) as its pivot, point of application, and center of reference.

Find the Self within the action — not an objective self which does something and is just another thing — this is the next adjuration.

That Self cannot be personalized:

> *Verse 183.* The mental-vesture (of the self) certainly cannot be the highest Self, on account of its having a beginning and an end, because it has changes, because it has the nature of pain, and because of its objectivity. What sees is certainly not something seen, on account of the very nature of the what is seen (as being a restriction of seeing).

Comment. The Self — our consciousness — looks at, watches, and observes our mental operations, just as the mind observes (by feeling and by seeing) the position and movements of the bodily limbs. It is to be noted that we see only because of obstruction to sight. For example, we see the wall because it stops our seeing — if it were perfectly transparent we could not see it at all, and the same applies to everything else. Although seeing by sight is thus not-seeing, a partial blockage of sight, and thinking by the mind is similarly a process of not-knowing, there has to be a see-er, which is our consciousness (see-er-ness) even to see the not-seeing — which, after all, is the "objective" world. It is the See-er that we know ourselves to be. We call it "I," but there is not it-ness about it at all. Let people know themselves as this, and they may save themselves thousands of years of largely miserable and discontented existence.

The reason for this is that there is a step up, from manas-outlook to buddhi-outlook, and then even another, to self-outlook, or as the modern favorite expression is, orientation. This is not spectacular or dramatic. It answers the simple question: "Where do you find yourself today?" Some are even below the mental.

CHAPTER 8

THE USE OF BUDDHI (HIGHER MIND)

In the group of verses to which we have now come the author shows us that even the faculty of understanding (buddhi) or higher mind — perhaps we should say highest mind — is not our very self. It is not uncommon to hear people speak of higher and lower mind, but I think we may clarify the matter still more by a triple distinction — the lower mind, the higher mind and the highest mind. The lower mind will then be all that storage chamber of memories or mental pictures of past experience; the higher mind will be the logical capacity, comparing, classifying, and inferring; the highest mind will be that which evaluates the things so known from the standpoint of their benefit to life (one's own or that of others) and therefore chooses what to do and even what to think about (or feel about) at any given time. Perhaps this is specially evident in spare moments — consider the psychological question to oneself: "What do I think about at those times when I am not called upon to attend to anything?" Even the highest mind (buddhi) is not really oneself: —

> *Verse 184.* The buddhi, with its perceptive and active faculties (indriyas) and its various forms has the character of being the doer (or actor). It is the sheath (or covering or body) of knowing (vijñāna). It is the cause of a man's series of incarnations (sansāra).

Comment. It is the function which causes the distinction of subject and object (I and thou, or I and it). There is a distinction between the terms sañjñā, or knowing as such, and vijñā, distinguishing an object, and — by contrast — oneself, the subject of the experience of objects. The function is concerned with the contents of the field of objects (including even the Self when thought of as something, even as an "experiencer"), and, as it has its active side as well as its receptive side, it proceeds to action with reference to them, through the body (with its sense and action organs), the feelings or emotions, (which give strong relations to particular objects), and the lower and higher minds.

It is to be carefully noted — a very subtle matter — that even the common notion of the "I" (the self-image) is a product of this function, and is not the essential "I" or self that we feel without naming.

> *Verse 185.* This knowing of the objective is a form of matter (a piece of machinery or a body in the world), a power which is a reflection of pure consciousness (chit). Strongly and constantly it thinks of "I" in the dense and other bodies (koshas) as having knowledge and action.

Comment. This verse shows how this "fine body" or covering of the self is (a) not the self, though it (b) thinks itself to be the self, in all the bodies — that is, whether materially observing or acting, whether feeling, remembering, thinking or even "knowing."

We have to notice that thinking is not knowing. Thinking is a process of getting to know. It is somewhat analogous to walking. You walk to get somewhere, and when you arrive you stop walking. Similarly, you think to get knowledge, and when you arrive you stop thinking. Knowledge is different from thinking (as buddhi from manas). There is a sort of "click" which marks the change and so sometimes people will slap the thigh or clap the hands, and exclaim, "Ah, now I see — or know."

Buddhi is therefore more like perceiving than thinking.

> *Verse 186.* This is without beginning *in* time. It is the living being (jīva), the very being of ego, which carries on the common business of this collection (of being and things, or subjects and objects — the world). According to previously acquired tendencies (from time to time) it causes actions, both meritorious and unmeritorious, with their effects.

> *Verse 187.* It has experience according to various kinds of conditions of birth. It comes and goes, down and up. Belonging to this knowledge-sheath (vijñāna-māyā-kosha) also are the waking, dreaming and deep-sleeping states and the experience of pleasures and pains.

> *Verse 188.* This knowledge-sheath (vijñāna-kosha) constantly supposes that the qualities, duties and actions of the stages of life, and pertaining to the body, etc. are "mine." It is very splendid (as compared with the other "koshas") on account of its effective closeness to the Self-which-is-beyond (parātman); hence it is a deceptive appearance (upādhi) of that (Self) — (only) an idea of self that slithers along wanderingly (in the field of incarnation).

Comment. The knowledge-sheath or knowledge-covering or knowledge-body (though the word "body" has too much association with the material or physical body for it to be very safely used for the covering-composed-of-ideation) is the highest of the sheaths in that it is the nearest to the very consciousness. It is in the field of duality, subject-object relationship, and so in its activity the "I" is a "thou" — an object, though a subjective object. In this field of subject and objects even the subject is something seen in thought. You say: "I am so-and-so." There is a nomination or defining and thereby an objectivating of the self in thought. This vijñāna or distinguishment is usually translated "knowledge" but it is still error. In this manner our best knowledge is not-knowledge just as our sight is not-seeing (as already explained, we see the wall because it blocks our vision and prevents full seeing).

It must not be supposed, however, that when the un-relative consciousness, which is the knowing of Self by self, is seen or found, the vijñāna-self disappears. It can be there also, but it is known for what it is and then it does not usurp the place of the pure consciousness. This remark applies to all the sheaths (or bodies). They *are* objective. They have been made, and will persist until they are unmade. The whole business of action is objective. It is an illusion — like one's face seen in a mirror. For the mirror-face to be seen there has to be a real face, and even if you do smash the mirror the real face remains. This simile is defective, of course, and the koshas (bodies) are positive objective creations, or forms shaped by *action*. Therefore the guru, if he knows the Self (as he is supposed to), knows also his incarnate instrument (kosha) but does not mistake it for himself. It is believed that some day he will give it all up (and "go to the para," as the expression is) but that will be voluntary, as well as the fulfillment of his duty (dharma) to all the other "thous" with whom he has been concerned. Some people put it that he must "pay off all his karma," even if he is liberated in consciousness. All his actions will be unselfish and so not karma-making (karma-making being only making something for one's separate self, or rather idea of oneself).

This verse (188) speaks of nearness or closeness to the parātmā or parātman or paramātman (all the same word). This we see in the course of evolution — action, emotion, thought are progressively "nearer" to the Self, or less obscuring, and when the thought includes "thous" it is "nearer" than when it includes only "its." So it is more "shining" and less obscuring. All along the way there is, of course, only one light of consciousness — that of the parātmā, as stated in the next verse.

> *Verse 189.* This light made-of-knowledge (vijñāna-māyā) it is which shines forth in the life-forces (prānas) in the heart. Although existing (really) above (all duality of subject and object), the Self, standing in the disguise (upādhi of vijñāna), becomes the doer and experiencer.

Comment. In this verse the author indulges in a little symbolism. "The heart" stands for the center of recognized self-consciousness and the life-forces for all the functions, including the mental as well as the vital. The words doer (or actor) and experiencer indicate the mind of error which exists in the self-recognition when the knowing is thus centered. Hence this covering is called a deception or masquerade (upādhi) instead of a kosha. This is what happens when one rises even above the mental or logical operations (of manas) and operates the understanding or the love ("I am the doer" or "I am the lover") which is vijñāna or buddhi. In modern terms love (true love), which is harmony, is the *way* to unity, but is not unity. ("No man cometh unto the Father but by me," saith the Christ, or anointed man or spirit of love). So:

> *Verse 190.* Itself having fallen into the condition of buddhi (or vijñāna), by the defect (or fault) or errone-

ous identification with that, which is other than itself although it is the "self" in all (beings), it regards itself differently from (that) Self — just as (in the case of) the clay and the pot.

Verse 191. Through the power of its connection with a disguise (upādhi) the Supreme Self exhibits the character and the qualities of that disguise — just as fire, which is formless (takes on) the forms of iron, away from its own nature (which is) beyond (all that).

Comment. The self has also been compared to an actor playing a role or part and being quite mistaken by himself and others, for that person.

There is one principle clearly brought out in all these verses. What the West usually regards as creation is really demolition, or what it regards as addition or building-up is really deduction, or what it regards as revealing is really hiding. The universe is not built up from immortal material elements but material elements are (each of them) partial denials of the perfect element which would have the qualities of all of them, and all at once, similarly, the perfect life. And finally, the perfect all, in which there is no distinction of each, and there is perfect unity — not union, but unity — and there is no sort of separateness of all. Some cows are red-brown, some white, some black; any one that is red, or black, or white, is not-cow, or imperfect cow, to the extent that it excludes the others.

Another thought applied to the same truth is that of veiling. A mesh-like veil before the face of the Absolute is the first creation (creation as doing, being really undoing or separation), another mesh over that is the second creation, and so on. Then the net result of all the creations is still the same face, but all spread out "in space and time," so that *all* and *each* are both the same face, for there is nothing else but That Face.

Interruption. At this point the pupil interrupts the teacher with a question (verses 192 and 193). The pupil says:

Verse 192. Whether the existence of the Supreme Self as a living being (jīva) be due to an error or otherwise — still, on account of the beginning-lessness of the disguise (or semblance, upādhi) of it, no end (also) of the beginningless is possible.

Verse 193. Therefore of that existence as a living being (jīva), the revolving is also permanent. It cannot be reversed. Tell me, then, revered teacher, how liberation from it is possible.

Explanation. The teacher now replies in eight verses, which I shall summarize to save space. This reply begins and ends with the smashing assertion that the supposed relation between the ātman and the jīva is nothing but "false knowledge" or delusion, is not rational or logical (not pramānaka), and is produced by delusion, (mohita-kalpanā). When a rope is mistaken for a snake, and then the truth is discovered, what becomes of the snake? (One is reminded of Buddha's statements, as expressed in English by Sir Edwin Arnold in his beautiful poem *The Light of Asia:* "Delusion fashioned it," and "Ye are not bound"). Error or ignorance is beginning-less, says the teacher, but it certainly ceases when the truth is realized, as in waking up from dream.

The teacher here instructs the pupil in one of the technicalities of Indian Logic, namely "previous non-existence" (prāg-abhāva). The previous non-existence (e.g., of a house before it is built) ceases (when the house is built), but it never began. So the jīva simply is not real; it does not really exist. Somebody is making a mistake. It is all children's toy castles. The little girl's doll is not a baby. Yet we may say the delusion has value, like the doll. But the truth will be known only when it is known, and that will be when the error is overcome.

After thus describing the error the teacher proceeds, in verse 200, etc. to explain how we can proceed to remove the error.

CHAPTER 9

THE REMOVAL OF ATTACHMENT

We come now to a series of verses in which the teacher informs the pupil how to remove the error which led the conscious unit into repeated attachment to limited things and consequent dependence upon them. Briefly it is by knowledge.

It is to be remembered that this "error," which has been carried along from our past into our present is not merely an error in idea, but also in action, for a world has been built by us collectively, and each one's own limited portion of it has been built individually in this way. Thus there is "the world" and there is "my world" — that portion of the world in which I find myself involved as a result of my action ("my karma").

We may put it that I have built a house, in which I now live. I have overlooked the fact that I have wings, and so I am hemmed in by floors and stairways and passages and have to plod up and down and in and out of the various parts of this restricting maze. So — (1) let me stop making more confusion and bondage, and (2) let me unmake what has been made, and (3) let me in that unmaking find my wings. For each of these three processes correct knowledge is required. The teacher says:

> *Verse 202.* Withdrawal comes about by means of correct knowledge, and not otherwise. In the opinion of the Scriptures, this correct knowledge is perception of the oneness of ātman and Brahman.

Verse 203. Then, only by correct discernment of ātman and non-ātman it is accomplished. Therefore discrimination should be done between the personal self (pratyag-ātman) and the true self (sad-ātman).

Verse 204. Just as in the case of very muddy water, when the mud is removed, the water shines clearly, so also the Self in the absence of faults shines forth clearly.

Comment. It has become a habit for one to say "I" with reference to all the tools of activity which we have hung around ourselves. We say, "I dig with this spade," but should say, "My hands dig with the spade" — I direct the hands. There should be a clear discrimination between the hand and the I — while the work is going on. This may be difficult, because of old habit of thought. It is here that meditation is useful. Observing the error again and again in imagination (in imaginative meditation) one weakens the old wrong habit. As a result of this the true idea will come up again and again until it is there on all occasions of action.

Then comes the second stage or depth of knowledge. We say, "I desire the hole to be dug." Careful; careful. It is desirable that a hole should be dug, because . . . What, then, desires? The body again.

But there are *reasons* for digging, for eating, etc. — So "I think." Another meditation, please, with plenty of imagination, not mere words and abstractions. But what thinks? Body again; it is a process as definite and limited by mental structure as an arm or a leg. Given the data, this thinking is a push-button business. There is the I and the thinking, but no "I think."

I have mentioned before an occasion on which a guru (teacher) requested a pupil to walk to the far end of the room and back, and after this had been done, suddenly asked: "What were you doing just now? Were you walking?" After a little reflection, and going over the occasion in imagination, the pupil could say, "No, *I* was not walking. *I* was watching the body walk."

Later the question will arise: "Who or what is this I?" But this is *not permissible*. The I or self is at last to be known only *by itself*. So the teacher now speaks of the newly known reality which the self is as bursting-forth (sphuta). It itself "bursts forth." It is not to be *thought* of as like somebody (an answer to "who?"), nor like something (an answer to "what?").

> *Verse 205.* In the removal of the faults there is the bursting forth by the real self. The result of this (action of removal) is correct orientation. Therefore the removal from the true self of anything, (such as thinking) "I am holy", etc., should certainly be done.

> *Verse 206.* Hence, this Supreme Self (Parātman) cannot be what is called the-body-made-of-knowledge (vijñāna-māyā-kosha) — because that has various forms, because of its deadness, because of its being a cause of sub-divisions, because of its objectivity, and because of its changeability. (To think that) this non-eternal is the eternal is not approved.

Comment: The student may remember that in the teaching it has already been stated that there are *five* bodies or coverings or sheaths one within the other. These may be translated freely as, (1) the material, (2) the vital, (3) the mental, (4) the moral, and (5) the spiritual. What I have here called the moral is the body-made-of-knowledge (vijñāna-māyā-kosha), because its knowledge is not knowledge about things (which is the business of the mental body) (the mano-māyā-kosha) but knowledge of life. As such it is concerned — in terms of evolution — especially with "coherence" or integrity, not with "heterogeneity" or additions. As such its wisdom will direct the body into ways of health (bodily integrity), and the mind into considerations of rationality, which again is integral thinking, or mental health.

The teacher has just said that the "I" cannot be even the moral. He now will go still further and say that it cannot be the body-made-of-joy (ānanda-māyā-kosha), the fifth body in the series: —

> *Verse 207.* The body-made-of-joy (ānanda-māyā-kosha) is the form which is the body that is kissed by the reflection of the supreme joy (ānanda), and which arises in the darkness, has the qualities of affection, etc., and is the source of the obtainment of rightly desired (su-ishta) objects. When there is the accomplishment of merit, the form-of-joy itself (i.e. the ānanda-māyā-kosha) which is called its product, shines forth and in that case all good people, by merely having that body, have joy without effort.

> *Verse 208.* It is in the sleeping state that there is the strong activity of the body-made-of-joy (ānanda-māyā-kosha). It is only slightly so in the dream and waking states, (and then) on account of the seeing, etc., of what is desired.

Comment. Shankarāchārya, our author, here rises to great poetic heights, and adopts a prolonged rolling and sonorous meter suited to the subject (beginning with a long line of 20 syllables). The word "kissed" is a literal translation (chumbita). Of the three higher bodies (koshas) we may say that the mental body looks down upon and is affected by *the world,* the moral body looks levelly upon and is affected by *other living beings,* and the spiritual body looks up to and is affected by what is *beyond*—the Brahman. These three (manas, buddhi, and the human ātman) constitute that portion of the human being which in the West has come to be called "the Higher Self." The three parts of it look down, look level, and look up, respectively, and, of course, they are all in operation *in some measure* all the time in every one of us. It is not to be thought that any of them is still to be acquired.

It is Brahman, of course, that is the supreme joy. In Vedānta he is also the supreme reality and the supreme consciousness (three inseparables, really one). This too is the real self of the individual person beyond all the koshas. In the *Bhagavad-Gītā* the individual is described as a *share* (ansha) of Brahman. This is the real I all the time, but when a man *thinks of himself* he usually identifies himself with the body, the emotions, the thinking mind, and so on. This is wrong knowledge. Even that body-made-of-joy is still not the self, (the real ātman). The aspirant to real knowledge must not accept even that reflected joy as really himself. It has a limited coming up in consciousness when there is merit (which is when all the other koshas are lined-up under this and are living to their maturity and fullness, but *under* the guidance of this kosha). This is not something to be sought for or to be worked for. This joy takes care of itself and comes of itself (bursts forth) because of the reflection or being "kissed."

> *Verse 209.* This body-made-of-joy is certainly not the Supreme Self, because of its being a covering (vesture — upādhi), on account of its being a form of matter, on account of its being something made (or produced), on account of its being produced by good deeds, and on account of its association with the assemblage of forms.

> *Verse 210.* When the five koshas are eliminated as

indicated in the scriptures — in that elimination the
superior observer (ātman), having the nature of knowledge, is left.

Comment. What was said about the vijñāna-māyā-kosha
(body-made-of-knowledge) in verse 206, namely that it is
not the Supreme Self, for various reasons, is now repeated
with variations here with respect to the ānanda-māyā-kosha:—

Verse 211. That very ātman which is self-shining, is
distinct from the five koshas, is the witness of the three
states, is not a product, and is unstained and always
joyful — that should be known by the wise man by
means of his own selfness (not by any kosha or body).

Explanation. Regarding the five bodies of man.

Although first propounded in the old Upanishad books of
India perhaps 3000 years ago, the five-fold classification of
man is very appropriate in connection with our modern
studies of man. Man is still a being having a body (with
sense-organs and muscles, and a vital system), desires or
emotions, thoughts, ethical impulses (good-will or love to
others) and will-power or decision. Modern elementary books
on psychology still give us three functions of the mind as will,
feeling, and thought. The word feeling is ambiguous, as it
can cover enjoyment for both (a) bodily pleasures and (b)
feeling for others. In Sanskrit we have two words — kāma
commonly used for bodily pleasures and desires, prema for
the love of others (which, of course, has many degrees and
varieties, according to circumstances, so that we have compassion at one end of the scale and devotion or worship at
the other, with friendship in the middle).

The point I want to make here is that all five are all
present in all people (except perhaps madmen), but the top
two (love and the spiritual impulse) are *relatively* feeble, im-

mature, or undeveloped in most. Some students picture themselves as down below, so to speak, and aspiring to receive
something to be "brought down" from the higher self. Thus
they habituate themselves to the below. Really, even as
persons they are all the five. When we think we *are* thought;
when we love we *are* love. That principle of our being is then
in action. Thus, buddhi is not something "up there," "above
us," etc., and the student should habituate himself to being
that, by being intelligently and consciously ethical at all times
and toward everybody he deals with. Many people have
plenty of capacity for feeling for others, but they simply
forget, out of old habit. In India, this mistake has never been
made. Any mention of a "new birth" or an "anointing" in
this respect means only that the buddhi has jumped into a state
of prominence or leadership among the faculties of a man.

Some modern writers speak of seven instead of five
principles of man, but they cover the same ground. Thus, in
the Blavatsky books we have body divided threefold (including "etheric double" and vitality) then mind divided into
kāma-manas and manas proper, then buddhi and the human
ātman. It makes no difference, as all the "principles" can be
subdivided.

CHAPTER 10

WHAT REMAINS?

The pupil now poses a question (in verse 212), wanting to know what is left when the five coverings or instruments or vehicles are eliminated, that is, regarded as not being one's real self. He asks what sort of thing remains to be known as oneself.

The reader will perhaps recall the five coverings (1) the dense body, (2) the vitality body, (3) the mind, (4) the higher mind or intelligent "heart" and (5) the I-making consciousness. These are, in Sanskrit, sthūla, prāna, manas, buddhi and ahankāra.

The Guru (teacher) now replies:

> *Verse 213-4*. You speak rightly, O learned one. You are clever in reasoning. That by which all these constructs — the I-maker and the (four) others are experienced, and also, subsequently, their absence, that is not (something) itself experienced. You should understand that *that* Self is to be known (only) by *the* most subtle understanding.

> *Verse 215*. That by which the seer (of the five — the I-maker and the other four) is known *must* exist, (since) when there is no experience of anything, experiencing cannot be spoken of.

Comment. The Guru enters upon the theme that subject and object can never be the same, or of the same kind. The same principle enters into the modern question of evolution of organic forms. There has to be something which is not *passive* (that is, the principle of consciousness) in order that there may be a response and that adaptation of environment (as when a man makes a fire or builds a house) may take place. We are to see in the next verse how the problem is solved, how we *can* know consciousness even though consciousness is not an *object* of knowledge.

> *Verse 216.* This is self-witnessing being, so it is experienced by itself. Hence the individual self (pratyak-ātman) is obviously the Supreme Self and no other.

Comment. We can have empathy or sympathy with other conscious creatures. We can and do infer from their actions and speech that they have consciousness like ours, and we instinctively respond to their pains and pleasures, as if they were our own, and feel for them, glad to see their joy and sorry to see their suffering. But we can never — try as we will — enter into their actual consciousness.

We know only our own consciousness. And as we do not know anything but what is in our consciousness, there has arisen a philosophic theory called solipsism — the idea that only I exist, the rest could be a dream of mine (like that of the Chinese philosopher who did not know whether he was a man dreaming of a butterfly, or a butterfly dreaming of a man).

The problem is entirely solved by the hypothesis that there is only one of us. This is a wonderfully fruitful subject for meditation and indeed contemplation. It is entirely in accord with the conclusion in verse 216, that the individual self *is* the Supreme Self and not other, and therefore that the Supreme Self is *all* these. There is only one *consciousness as such*. Would it help to call it the divine puppeteer?

Perhaps this is what Jesus was talking about; calling it Father and saying "I and the Father". Even to a crowd of common people who threatened to stone him, and would have done so had he not escaped from them, he repeated and confirmed, "Ye are gods."

In the next verse, the Guru says that however we may involve ourselves in the passing show it is the same pure consciousness that is operating and makes it all possible. He will add that this consciousness is existence and joy or, as some have translated it, bliss — which however is too subjective a word for my taste, as it seems to give the impression of something rather retiring and exclusive of the fullness of life, while really it must know itself and be itself even in the midst of the crowd.

> *Verse 217.* That which is very clearly showing itself in (all the three states of) waking, dreaming and deep (or good) sleep; that which, inwardly formed, is constantly showing in various ways as "I," "I"; that which is the producer of various forms (or objects) and looking at them confronts the I-am intelligence (or consciousness), showing as the always joyful conscious self — know in your heart that this is yourself.

Comment. In this verse the author tries to show how the Self or consciousness may be directly viewed, while in the next verse (218) he describes how the unthinking person misses this direct vision:

> *Verse 218.* A foolish person, looking at the image of the sun reflected in the water in a jar, thinks it to be the very sun. Just so also a senseless person, through misapprehension, regards the *expression* of the (pure) consciousness located in the body (upādhi) as "myself."

Verse 219. (But) setting aside the jar, the water and the reflection of the sun which has gone into that — all of them — the sun (itself) is discerned. In that manner, by the wise man (is seen) the self-illuminated illuminator of the three (states).

Comment. Following this, the guru proceeds to show how freedom from sin (or error) and taint ensues, and then liberation from the bondage of reincarnation.

CHAPTER 11

THE ATTAINMENT OF FREEDOM

The teacher (guru) in our text now goes on to show how *freedom* or *liberation* can be attained. There is no doubt that anybody who pauses to realize his present position as a living being must admit to himself that he is a *prisoner*. This is so, regardless of whether he finds his life pleasant or unpleasant. The question then arises, by what or by whom is he imprisoned? By anything in the world? By other people? By God? By himself — by his own error or folly? The guru answers: —

Verses 220-2. (1) Having set aside the body and the (ordinary) intelligence, and even the *reflection* of the pure consciousness;

(2) Having come to know, in his deep, inner intelligence (or, we may say, intuition, which is interior perceptive direct intelligence) the true nature of himself, as the See-er (or consciousness, or observer) — the Self (the I), which is the indivisible Knowledge which lights up everything, whether real or unreal (or actual or false), and is constant, always present, pervading everything, very subtle, and without inside-and-outside (without duality), and admits of nothing other than Self:

(3) A man becomes free from fault, passion, death (which reincarnation involves); he is a "lamp of joy," Self-illumined. How could anything frighten him?

For óne desiring liberation there is no other means for (gaining) liberation from bondage to (the ordinary state of) being, than this reaching of the truth about oneself.

Verses 223-4. The means to release from (ordinary) being (i.e. incarnation) is perception of one's non-separateness from God (Brahman). By this the wise man attains Brahman, the non-dual, joy.

He who knows (this) does not return again to the cycle (of births and deaths), having become divine (Brahman). Therefore the perfect non-separateness of the Self (Atman) from Brahman is to be observed.

Comments on (1). There are several ways of setting aside the body, etc. These things — the body, the emotions, the memory, the reason, the mental picture of oneself as something in and of the world — are usually inspected dispassionately one by one until each is seen and felt to be "not myself" but something that is possessed or used. The whole bag of tricks is seen to be no different from, let us say, a finger. One teacher recommended his students to begin with this — hold the finger up, look at it, realize that "such a thing cannot be I." It may be considered that *all* these things are bundles of habits, and so are material — the material being that which does not change of itself from moment to moment, but carries the past into the present, and is therefore not alive. I am alive because I infuse some change into or among these things, if not change of substance or of form, at least change of relationships. Insomuch however, as my changes of them — my actions upon them — from moment to moment of my living are themselves determined by any of those things, my living is negative, perhaps this comes about through desire for them, perhaps through fear of them. This negativeness is the acceptance of bondage, except when I positively accept them — for example, using a pen at the moment and not a sword — and in so doing accepting the pen as pen.

What, then, is real or positive living? It is the decision, with reference to action or non-action in a particular case, which has its motive in the *depth* of oneself. What then is this, and how is it to be recognized? That depth is fullness of being, the fount of moreness of being. Acting positively means keeping this conduit open, so that in each decision or act there is *more life*. Jesus — who evidently knew what he was talking about — stated this as the purpose of his teaching, "That ye shall have *life* more abundantly." In any moment in which we are expressing an increase of life we are bringing something in from the divine potential or source. There is newness in this.

This is a matter of quality of living, not of quantity. More possessions are not more life, nor is more pleasure (of eating, drinking, jumping, etc.) nor is more knowledge (information) as to what is going on in the world. There is a newness of life in the vegetable above the mineral, in the animal above the vegetable, in the human above the animal — and similar stages are again seen relatively in the lives of various sorts of human beings.

Well, then, there comes a time when a man may by his own volition pass from the human to the divine, in this life in this world, and that means he releases himself from the acceptance of bondage in every small decision of his life — release from fear and from the kind of desire which is attachment. He begins to see the use or value of everything, the good in everything, which is the "God" in everything. It is not without significance that we instinctively accept the opinion that a baby cannot attain liberation. The child must become mature. The senses, the observing and remembering intelligence, the reflective intelligence or reason, the response to life in others, the impulse to harmony and unity — all are expressions of moreness of being, from the fount, or potential, or divinity or fullness. Great surprise was felt when a certain guru in India raised the question as to whether a pet cow (equal to a pet dog or cat in the West) could attain liberation. The answer was, of course, "No." There must be the development of the mentality or harmony with objects, and of love, or harmony with others, and then in turn there arises the desire for non-separation from what is loved — or unity. It becomes apparent then that the longing for unity of being or consciousness is the way to liberation from bondage. Behind the variety in oneself one then discovers the uniting principle of the pure consciousness, which is the same as the state of Brahman, the non-dual. It is worth reflecting upon in this connection that the very word "Brahman" means the grower or expander. That is God in the world, not separate from it. I do not know what the *word* "God" means, etymologically.

Comment on (2). The Self as See-er, Knower, is always present when there is any knowing, etc. Without this there would be no response to environment, and no evolution, or increase within.

Comment on (3). And so freedom is not escape but mastery, is not separateness but harmony and unity, is not desire and fear but knowledge and love. Liberation is not the end of a sequence; it is not for the future; it is here and now and always, but one has to be receptive of it.

And, finally, life and joy are the same thing. We see this even relatively; pain and sorrow are indications of some restriction of life. And life is being — the act of being, or being — doing — being. So being, consciousness (or knowing) and joy are all one.

Comment. The next point in question, after one has obtained a perception of one's own pure consciousness and realized that this is one's own very being, one's own self, is: "Why does the guru bring Brahman in?" The answer is that most people have heard about Brahman through the scriptures long before they ever thought about finding themselves. They have pictured a Being or God who is the creator (source) of the world, is the preserver of it and could be or will be the destroyer or dissolver of it all. He now learns that this God *operates through life,* that all living beings are the functioning of God, each in its own measure. Let us see by some examples how this is so. The formation of the hand of a monkey results from the efforts of the monkey to take hold of a branch of a tree, or a fruit. We can see also the earlier stages of this in the case of a squirrel, in its use of its forepaws. A wooden carved statue of a squirrel or a monkey does not evolve; this occurs only when there is life. Even a plant is gropingly doing the same thing — enjoying life and (unknowingly) seeking more life (not in quantity but in quality). Increased quantity without change leads to boredom.

Well, then, — to jump to the top — sooner or later a man realizes that what he enjoys is life, not the things he uses or handles, not the body which is, so to say, an elaborate hand, a tool which has been gradually formed by use. This man has come to the point where he has a mind as well as a hand or a body, and now he can carve wood — he can adapt the environment to himself, whereas the less developed creatures (which show "lessness" of life as compared with man) are still adapting themselves to their environment. And while using the words "himself" and "themselves" in this connection we must notice that they mean the body, for as the body is the instrument or tool for dealing with the outside world (which, be it noted, is only the conglomerate result of the activities of all the other living beings, as of this date) the man, or monkey or other creature, thinks of himself or itself as the body, as most people still do. Most people have come to the point of thinking "my body," without yet distinguishing the two elements in this statement—the owner and the owned, the self and the body. Then they think of "my mind," without clarity until they come to study the two elements in the statement, especially the significance of "my."

This statement is, then, that all forms are the product of life. Go back behind the vegetable. We have then what is usually called substance, and is generally regarded as completely negative, and spoken of as mineral or even element. This will not do. Here too we have life expressing itself, but more simply than the vegetable. But people say minerals are all uniform, all gold is exactly the same, or all atoms of gold are exactly the same. But they are still gold, not tin, and are very stubborn about maintaining their status, and resisting what to them would be death of their body, very much, essentially, as a man does. There *is* no substance — only life status and relationships of the "life-atoms." Our environment, then — mine and yours — consists of all other lives with their relative powers, or degrees of power and bondage, their expressions of themselves at present or up to this date.

So Brahman or God turns out to be life, not another body like a magnified man or a magnified mind. The student or reader, therefore, has to be requested by the guru at this point to change his idea about the God of life. I suppose something of this may have been in St. Paul's mind when he adjured his church or assembly members to try to rise to "the stature of the fullness of Christ" — not the fullness of the stature, but the stature of the fullness. We may think, I believe, of the Christ as the spirit of love or harmony gradually seeping into men as their response to it (use of it in body and mind) opens the conduit, and that it will then lead on to unity, which is the hidden core of love or harmony and acts as its harbinger in consciousness. Similarly, the mind has its secret core of love, which will sprout in due season, for the putting forth of it contains a desire for presence or possession, without which it will do no forthgoing. There is no mental activity without interestedness.

Therefore our author has said, in the verse just translated: "Perfect non-separateness of the Self from Brahman is to be perceived." "Should be perceived" would also be a good translation. He consequently now proceeds, in a series of verses (225 to 239) to make statements about Brahman. To save space, I shall not translate these verses in full, but will give a list of the characteristics of Brahman which occur in the verses: —

Verses 225 to 240. (Extracts). Brahman is:

Truth.

Knowledge.

Unchanging joy.

The Beyond.

Unseparate from individual life.

Without inside or outside.

The real.

The Supreme non-dual.

Only repository of knowledge of the truth which is the ultimate aim.

All this universe, which appears variously only through ignorance.

Completely free from the defects of thought.

Always the same, as a jar is always clay.

The real source and substance of everything.

That without which nothing is.

Not in beings, nor containing beings.

The reality even in mistaken conceptions, as when mother-of-pearl is mistaken for silver, or a rope for a snake.

Pure.

Stainless.

Peaceful.

Other than all the products of māyā.

Beginningless and endless.

Non-active.

Eternal.

Without parts.

Unmeasurable.

Formless.

Unmanifest.

Indescribable.

Immutable.

Self-revealing.

Without distinction of knower, knowing and known.

Infinite.

Unimaginable.

Essentially one whole indivisible consciousness.

Unremovable.

Unpossessible.

Beyond the scope of mind and speech.

The full.

The great.

The I.

Comment. These collected terms of praise are embodied in flowing verses which help in the mood of meditation. Each statement contains some error or inadequacy, but at the same time prevents some old error from holding on. In addition there is a prevailing feeling of devotion and glad gratefulness.

Still, it is all a preparation for the next group of verses, which form a yoga-meditation technique for realizing the universal significance and states of oneself. Just as one thing is as it is because of everything else, so also everything else is what it is because oneself is what one is.

CHAPTER 12

"That" and "Thou"

Now we begin on verse 241, and after a few preliminaries will come to what I have called "The Ten Meditations on 'That thou Art'."

Verse 241. By the words "That" and "Thou" in the saying "That thou art" (Tat twam asi) again and again repeated by Scripture, the perfect unity of the two which are being spoken of — Brahman and the Self — when the two words are carefully used, is understood.

Verse 242. This does not mean, however, the unity of the two words as indicating characteristics opposed to each other — like the moon and the sun, a king and a dependent, a well and the ocean, or an atom and the greatest mountain (each pair being the same in essence, but different in minor points — i.e., both lights, both men, both reservoirs, both material objects respectively).

Comment. Brahman and the Self — (ātman or ātmā) — are thus of the same substance or essential nature. It is averred that the aspirant has the power to see or experience that sameness, to know it positively, not merely to reason about it. This experience is often called illumination or realization.

Verse 243. In the case of each pair, the distinction is produced by a limitation (upādhi). This (upādhi) is never in the real thing (or actual substance). In the case of (God) it is illusion (māyā) which is the cause of the (appearances called) mind, etc. In the case of the individual living being (jīva) the effects are the five sheaths (or bodies).

Comment. The word upādhi means "deceptive appearance." In the case of an ordinary human being the deception lies in the thought of oneself as the body, mind or ego (whether objective ego or subjective ego) and lack of realization of the Self, the "spark of the divine." By this we learn that the discovery of the Self does not involve unawareness of the upādhis called body, mind and ego; for just as you do not have to destroy your body in order to know your mind, so also you need not destroy your mind or your ego in order to know the Self. But just as we regard ourselves ordinarily as the mind using the body, or as the ego using mind and body, so the enlightened, united, or liberated man knows himself as pure Self even while using ego, mind, and body. Suicide *of any kind* (i.e. of body, feelings or mind) is not the way to liberation or Self-realization. It is to be understood, however, that when this liberation from illusion is arrived at there is no necessity for future incarnations except for the purpose of trafficking with other embodied egos in the general world of jīvas, or world of illusion.

Mention of māyā calls for a brief explanation also. It is that by which God allows us to deceive ourselves, as to both his nature and our own. This deception is positively played out or acted, forming a world of things and beings which are what they seem, though only temporarily, until the illusion is counteracted (the action undone). First there is an idea, which is always a limitation (all ideas are), and then there is action upon the idea, forming a thing or things. Desire or interest shuttles between idea and action. (All desires are thus also limitations.)

Verse 244. When the two appearances, God and the individual (jīva) are completely eliminated (as being upādhis) there is no God and no individual. In case of a kingdom and a king, or of a soldier and his weapon — in the removal of either of the pair there is no soldier or no king.

Comment. This is equal to saying that the Self which is known in realization is not *at all* like anything known before. It is *beyond* both subject and object, both of which are limitations. It is *not* a new subject to which both subject and object together have become a new combined object. It is completely outside or beyond the field of relations, or relative field. That is why this enlightenment can never be described, though there is plenty of testimony to its actuality or reality, nor can it be sought for — for seeking implies something being sought, and thus to some extent defined, if only as "not this." It will come "like a thief in the night." So the "not this" is only a rejection of error, not an indicator of any truth.

The next verse (245) refers to a statement in the *Brihadāranyaka Upanishad* (2, 3, 6) that the only appropriate reference to Brahman is as "Not this, not this." Brahman cannot be known by any comparison or qualification whatsoever. The Scripture does, however, permit the description or definition of Brahman as "The truth of truth."

Verse 245. The scriptural statement, "Now therefore, etc." (given above) itself wards off any imagining of duality in Brahmān. Thus from knowledge derived from the authority of Scripture the elimination of the two (upādhis) is likewise effected.

Verse 246. "Neither this nor this" is the truth — like the snake seen in a rope, and as (anything seen) in a dream. Having thoroughly removed "the seen" in this manner the unity of be-ing of the two can subsequently be really known (or realized).

Verse 247. Therefore for the successful understanding of the unbreakable unity of the two (Brahman and ātman) the two are to be well examined with their implications. Not merely by change of sense (jahat), nor by addition of sense (ajahat) but only by the combined significance of both is it to be understood.

Comment. By change of sense (jahat) we here mean such a case as, "The town is on the Ganges," by which it is meant that the town is beside the Ganges. Then by addition to sense (ajahat) we mean such a case as, "The roan wins the race," when the word "horse" is to be understood as being implied. These are called implications. Jahat and ajahat are definite technical terms in old Indian logical studies.

Verse 248. Oneness only is spoken of in *"This* is *that* Devadatta"* the portions having contrary meaning (i.e. this and that) being cast off. Similarly, in the saying "That thou art" (Tat twam asi) the contrary meanings in both (i.e., that and thou) are to be removed.

Verse 249. The undivided oneness of being of the Brahman and the Self has been ascertained by the wise after full study of what is implied. Thus by hundreds of great sayings (in the Scriptures) the unbroken unitary being of Brahman and Atman is announced.

Comment. In the next verse (250) there is again a reference to the *Brihad-āranyaka Upanishad* (3, 8, 8). Speaking of Brahman, the great sage Yajñavalkya says that Brahman is neither huge nor atomic, neither short nor long, etc., etc. . . . (ending) without inside or outside, neither eating nor being eaten.

Verse 250. "Not huge, etc." Thus having eliminated the unreal, this (declaration of unity) is self-evident, just as there is no argument about (the existence of) the sky. Therefore, set aside the common deceptive notion which holds to the Selfness (ātma-ness) of yourself (as commonly thought of; i.e., body, mind, etc.). Declaring "Brahman am I" with pure understanding, realize the truth that there is no division between yourself and the Self (ātman).

Comment. There is of course a certain danger even in speaking of the Self as the Self. You thereby objectify it, or stand it off as something to be looked at. Or you may, indeed, make the common error of looking up to it as a higher self, and so definitely accept yourself as settled into an upādhi. The pure consciousness must look at the pure consciousness, not in the distorting and limiting mirrors.

To save space I shall now summarize verses 251, 252, 253. They say that just as all pots are really clay, so everything (both objective and subjective) is Brahman, the only reality and self-existent substance, and you, too, are that. We now come to what I have called:

THE TEN MEDITATIONS ON "THAT THOU ART"

1. *(Verse 254.)* Far from social status, religious creed, family qualities and racial characteristics; without name, form, qualities and defects: the Brahman —

That *thou* art (Tat twam asi).

Ponder on this, inside thyself (bhavaya ātmani).

2. *(Verse 255.)* That which is the beyond, outside the range of words, yet within the range of the eye of unmired intelligence, a real existence without origin and compact of pure consciousness: the Brahman —

That *thou* art (Tat twam asi).
Ponder on this, inside thyself.

3. *(Verse 256.)* Unconnected with the "six waves," and not manifest to the organs of sense, but evident in the heart to the unified person, the Brahman —

That *thou* art (Tat twam asi).
Ponder on this within thyself.

Comment. The six waves are decay, death, hunger, thirst, sorrow, and illusion, called waves because of their superficiality and temporary nature. One is reminded of verses II, 14, and 15 of the *Bhagavad-Gītā:* "The encounters with the material (world), giving cold and heat and pleasure and pain, come and go. Bear patiently those impermanent (experiences), for he is fit for deathlessness to whom these do not cause anguish, the wise man, to whom pain and pleasure are similar." The word heart means, of course, not the physical organ, nor the chest cavity which is what is meant by "heart" in Sanskrit books generally, but the depths of one's consciousness of being.

4. *(Verse 257.)* The substratum of the world which is fashioned awry, having no basis other than itself, being without parts and without likeness to anything: the Brahman —

That *thou* art. (Tat twam asi).
Ponder on this, within thyself.

5. *(Verse 258.)* Devoid of birth, growing, maturing, decline, decrepitude, and destruction; indestructible; the cause of the production, preservation and destruction of the world: the Brahman —

That *thou* art. (Tat twam asi).
Ponder on this within thyself.

6. *(Verse 259.)* Undivided; without loss of its own characteristics; unmoving as an ocean without waves; eternally free; of undivided form: the Brahman —

That *thou* art. (Tat twam asi).
Ponder on this within thyself.

7. *(Verse 260.)* One being, yet the cause of many; without cause, yet the eliminator of other causes; not having the character of the series of causes and effects; self-existent; the Brahman —

That *thou* art. (Tat twam asi).
Ponder on this in thyself.

8. *(Verse 261.)* Without any mental process; not trifling; not expendable; without either decreasing or increasing; beyond (all); eternal; unfading happiness; stainless: the Brahman —

That *thou* art. (Tat twam asi).
Ponder on this in thyself.

9. *(Verse 262.)* The reality which mistakenly appears as if itself having many changes of name, form and quality, but itself being always unchanged, like gold: the Brahman —

That *thou* art. (Tat twam asi).
Ponder on this in thyself.

10. *(Verse 263.)* That than which no other is; beyond all other; essential unity of being, having the character of self (ātman); reality, consciousness and happiness; infinite; unchanging: the Brahman —

That *thou* art. (Tat twam asi).
Ponder on this in thyself.

II. *Comment*. The remark about gold in meditation 9 refers to all sorts of vessels and other objects made of gold. It is a common saying that the gold is still only gold and there is nothing else.

CHAPTER 13

MEDITATIONS ON "THAT THOU ART"

We now have brought our verses from the Chūdāmani to the high peak of the meditations on the sentence "That thou art" (Tat twam asi). After that comes a group of verses containing warnings against the dangers of egoism (ahankāra): (1) the danger of identification of oneself with the false self (the mentally built-up self of the present incarnation), and (2) the danger of identification of oneself with the feeling of self as "myself" as ruler of myself.

The latter danger is very subtle, and not very "practical politics" for those who have not yet got a thoroughly good view of the false self as the false self and not the real self.

And here another word of warning is necessary: the false self, or self-image as it is sometimes called, is not to be destroyed but is to be used in the business of bodily living, which constitutes the work of the present incarnation. It would mean that your awakening is constant; just as when you are driving your car and you know it is a car and that you are in the car and that you are driving the car, and that the car is a useful thing for your present business (that is busy-ness, a very appropriate word), so also in life you are aware of your false self or self-image as what it is, you are aware that you are in it, that you are driving it and that it is a useful thing for your present business. Then the myself that knows this false self will also come to know its own self (the ruler — Ishwara — of the false self; the god within that

I am) and will further know that it is going about its father's business and that itself and the father are one, and thus he will know that both himself and Brahman are one, and will be saying to himself, "Tat (That = Brahman) thou (the inner ruler) art." And it will not interfere with the business, or with the false self (derived from parents and education), but will irradiate them with clean power and joy (what some have called, too negatively as it seems to me, bliss).

What the business is — is another story. Let us go into that a little later, and in the meantime go back in our Chūdāmani verses and pick up the advice of the teacher (guru) as to how to use the car and make a good job of the business in hand. This advice appears in the first thirty verses of the Chūdāmani. In these we find described the "four means of attainment," sometimes translated by modern writers as "the four qualifications for treading the Path" — the Path (mārga) which is also described as consisting of three items: hearing (shravana), thinking (manana) and deeply contemplating beyond thought (nididhyāsana). When the last of these opens the door for insight, illumination, realization (many words are used for this) the person becomes "liberated while alive" (jīvanmukta). The last expression should be enough to warn us that the purpose and method are not of the nature of escape and retreat, but are rather of the nature of mastery and overcoming.

CHAPTER 14

THE LOOSENING OF THE FALSE SELF

The set of ten meditations on "That, thou art" is followed by twelve verses variously aimed at loosening the grip of the false self on our habit-thought of ourselves, so that the real Self may more and more be received by our minds, which will then — as a result of dwelling on these comparisons or similes — become obedient to the higher, and also become happier and stronger thereby, on account of a release from external worries and an intuitive refreshment from within. I will now translate these twelve verses:

> *Verse 265.* Having understood the real truth, just as it is explained, and standing constantly confident in that Self-nature — like a king with his army assembled — surrender the whole production unto Brahman.

Comment. There is aptness in bringing the idea of God (Brahman) in here, since the Self-nature (own ātman) now to be known has the character of independent self-being, not a product or a dependent. This is credited to others also, so our interest in the field of variety comes to be the welfare in that field. May I offer rather a crude example? A salesman, recommending some article, and having this insight, would have the welfare of the customer always in view.

> *Verse 266.* Brahman is present in the depths of the higher intelligence (buddhi) — the Reality, distinct from both being and non-being, absolutely without a second. Never again for him who here and now dwells with that

Self in the depth will there be entry into the body-cave
(womb).

Comment. It is only when the buddhic faculty is mature —
that wise understanding which involves love also — that the
real Self can begin to be consciously known. It will now be
consciously included in that assemblage of powers and possessions known as the self-image or personality-picture, and
then joyfully accepted as the ruler of all that little kingdom.

Reality beyond both being and non-being. To us there is
a reality of anything which exists; let us call it something.
Nothing also is real, as when we say, "There is nothing here."
Sometimes we call it space. But a something is not fully real,
because it excludes the reality called nothing. And a nothing
is not fully real, because it excludes the reality called something. The absolutely real is beyond these two categories.
Something is this absolutely real, but seen as it were through
a veil, and nothing is also this, also seen through a veil. So
their realities are still that same reality, but that absolute
reality cannot be known as "like" either of these. Buddha
had this difficulty in trying to speak of nirvāna. To describe
it as like anything, or within any class or definition, would
be wrong; so also it would be wrong to deny. Even to say
"it is" is wrong, and to say "it is not" is also wrong. The
mystery of love is deepened by this. I cannot say that you
are myself, also I cannot deny it. But the mystery is also
solved by the birth in due course of a consciousness of this
reality beyond the mind. It is then seen that the mind, like
the body, is an instrument competent only within its own
sphere. So one cannot anticipate the reality, nor ask for it.
Even the naming of it bars the realization.

Verse 267. Even when there is an understanding of the
truth, the strong and beginningless desire-habit (vāsanā),

expressed in "I am a doer and experiencer," is still the cause of the round of bodily living. By its removal with perseverance and by dwelling with inward insight on the Self, there is the thinning-away of the desire-habit (vāsanā) here and now, which the sages declare to be liberation.

Comment. Vāsanā is a curious word. Used in reference to material objects it means an odor, but in reference to human psychology it means the active habit-structure of the mind and its responses with automatic impulses of desire or aversion to circumstances as they arise, a view somewhat resembling our modern opinion of the subconscious mind. It consists of old responses lapsed into habit, ready to spring forth into action before our current faculties of thought, love, and decision get to work. It is this priority which has to be reduced and removed, for surely we still need our decisions and impulses for nearly all the routine part of our lives. Even the mind has its vāsanās of this kind. We are here enjoined to find ourselves as not the old mental picture of self developed from childhood, but as the witness of all that.

Verse 268. The condition "I" and "mine" in reference to the not-self of body, senses, etc.—this mental assumption (adhyāsa) is to be negated by the wise, by means of intentness upon one's real self.

Verse 269. Having known about one's own inner self, which is the witness of the higher intelligence (buddhi) and its evolvements, cast off the idea in not-self, by the correct formula expressed as "That, I am."

Verse 270. Having given up (1) the following of others, (2) dependence on the body, and (3) reliance on the scriptures, perform the removal of your assumption (adhyāsa).

Verse 271. Desire-habit (vāsanā) with regard to (1) people, (2) scriptures, and (3) body — or anything which will not lead to mastery.

Verse 272. For one who desires freedom from this prison-house of worldly life (sansāra), that strong triple desire-habit (vāsanā) is as an iron fetter binding the feet — say those who understand it. One who is freed from that obtains liberation.

Verse 273. The divine scent (vāsanā) of sandalwood, which is obscured by the horrible stink (vāsanā) produced by its contact with water, appears perfectly when the outer smell (vāsanā) is dispelled by rubbing.

Verse 274. The perfume (vāsanā) of the Supreme Self, which was besmeared with the dirt of endless long-lasting desire-habits (vāsanās) cooked-up inside (the mind), becomes clearly perceived by the strong rubbing (as it were) of wisdom — like the smell of sandalwood.

Verse 275. The perfume of the Self (ātman), diverted through the snares of the not-self desire-habits, of itself (again) becomes clearly evident when those are destroyed by means of constant devotion to the Self.

Verse 276. In whatever degree the mind becomes properly established, to that extent it gives up the outer desire-habits. When there is complete release from the desire-habits there is no longer any obstacle to realization of the Self.

CHAPTER 15

UNDERSTANDING SUPERIMPOSITION

We have come now to the series of verses which contain the reiterated formula: —

"Perform the removal of your own mistake (adhyāsa)."

There is a time-and-stress beat or rhythm in this formula in its original language which is very impressive, appealing and remindful. It goes:

"Swādhyāsāpanayam kuru."

(Swa, your own; adhyāsa, mistake of assumption; apanayam, the taking away or removal; kuru, do.)

The word adhyāsa is very much used in Vedānta philosophy. It means wrong ascription. When perceiving or thinking of anything, there is the attribution or ascription to it of something else seen or known previously, as, e.g., when a piece of rope on the ground is mistaken for a snake — a matter which may easily and frequently occur in an Indian village, especially when the people are going home along the field-paths in the dusk of evening.

Some writers prefer to translate the word adhyāsa as "superimposition," because — in the example cited — the idea of a snake is superimposed by the mind upon the perception of the piece of rope. Substitute the real "I" for the rope and the false self-image of oneself for the snake, and you have the obvious and common personal error — the mistake of ascription — which we are now trying to remove or overcome.

It is not only the Vedāntist author of the *Chūdāmani* who

emphasizes the importance of this piece of self-psycho-analysis. The great compiler of the Yoga-Sūtras, Patañjali, regards this error of mistaking for ourselves our mental picture of ourselves as *the prime cause* of all our troubles. This is so because it masks or hides the fact of our real being which is always present as our essential consciousness whenever we are conscious of anything, and is held by the sages and mystics (seers) of India to have its own untrammeled consciousness of itself even in the absence of any object. It is thus not a "subject" as over against objects; so it must be known as itself — the wonderful basis of our being — without any comparison or ascription to it of the character, quality or nature of anything otherwise known — which includes the subject as well as the object. It is obvious to all who look into the matter that we can regard our mind with its pictures as objective to our pure consciousness, just as we regard the body and its surroundings. Among those mind-pictures is the idea of "oneself" as a thing having a certain status in the world.

When it is asked of these writers and seers: "Why then are we apparently tied to this particular body and — shall we call it — mind or soul?" the answer is "Because of desire."

This answer brings to light another aspect of the adhyāsa. It need not be a total error, as in the case of the snake and the rope. It can be the mistake of the part for the whole. Someone says: "Look at that lamp on the shelf over there." You reply, "That's not a shelf; it's a table." He then looks again and says, "So it is. I did not notice the legs." This indicates that the error is never totally false. A snake is a sort of rope, is it not? Now our question is: "What is it about ourselves that we are missing?" The answer to that is, "The essential part." We could discuss separately whether it is the essential that gives rise to the non-essential or the non-essential that gives rise to the essential, but our business just now is to become very aware of that essential — not merely to infer or to imagine it, but to experience it, the consciousness of consciousness.

Now to the verses: —

> *Verse 277.* When the yogi is established in his own Self (ātman) the mind perishes, and there is the fading away of the desire-habits (vāsanās).
> Therefore: Perform the removal of your own mistake.

Comment. This sounds drastic, until we perceive that this verse is speaking of the culmination of the entire process of evolution of the person who is in the top class of the school, so to speak. The true yogin is one who seeks the unity. Here it speaks of one who has found it. It is then assumed that he has overcome the world (to use a Christian expression) and now is able to live in the realm of real being. Therefore he will not require reincarnation in this world of relativities, of lesser things.

> *Verse 278.* Sluggishness (tamas) perishes on account of both restlessness (rajas) and harmoniousness (sattwa). Then harmoniousness perishes by (its own) purity. Therefore, having resorted to sattwa:
> Perform the removal of your own mistake.

Comment. Tamas, rajas and sattwa refer to the three qualities of all material things, as expressing what we commonly call matter, energy and law in nature. These three terms occur constantly in the old philosophic and religious literature of India. As applied to the human constitution, tamas is not deadness but habit, including what are called the bodily desires or impulses or appetites. Rajas comes in when the mind seeks the objects of pleasure; then there is restless desire. This overcomes any inertia there may be, says our verse. When rajas arrives it is not enough to eat and satisfy the appetite and then wait until hunger arises again. No, there must be fancy foods to stir up the appetite un- naturally. In this way, with thousands of desires of various kinds, the rajas is increased and overcomes tamas. Sattwa, orderliness, which is often associated with thoughtfulness, overcomes rajas — "Hey, stop that nonsense; have regard for knowledge about things and causes and effects; seek health rather than exciting pleasures." It goes further and observes the values of things for the indwelling life of self and others, and then it is called goodness — morality and ethics.

The sattwa overcomes itself, so to speak, by its own purity or perfection. In its perfect calmness of understanding in relation to both things and other people, it can mirror the real self. It can turn inward to *understand* the part played by the spirit (real Self) or downward to deal with body and desires. But with reference to spiritual experience, thinking stops. Its own devotion dissolves it in reference to that. There is then more than ethic, which harmonizes with others in a union of living; there is the realization of the unity behind the harmony, the great joy of the unity of being in the midst of the variety of living. What happens then?

> *Verse 279.* Having understood quite definitely that momentum (prārabdha) will look after the body, depend upon firmness (will-power) and diligently —
> Perform the removal of your own mistake.

Comment. I have translated the word prārabdha as mo- mentum in this verse because it refers to karma or past actions continuing their effect into the present. The body has been set up, and now continues its own activities by the habit of nature, which is tamas. It is obvious that even if we are asleep or under an anesthetic the breathing, digestive, and similar processes continue by habit. According to Vedānta, when action is done what is called vikshepa (projection) comes into effect. Something is started and the energy goes on until expended. There is also some renewal as the fire (so to speak) is fed by air and fuel (food).

The idea is that every action that is done produces a disturbance which has to settle back to the place where the disturbance took place, as in the case of a stone thrown into a pond. Both the action and its effect are called karma. Since, then, a human being has started certain things he must meet their effects and cancel them out. So there is a great deal of desire and attachment which has brought about this body, and indirectly its environment and its adventures or apparently accidental experiences.

The man must deal with his own past; he cannot merely shrug it off. He has wrapped himself in this cocoon of house, furniture, clothing, books, and what not, and must burst it open, or burst out of it by becoming a better man than he was when he made it. This he does by dealing with his "karma" by will, love, and thought, and acting accordingly. While so doing his will, love, and thought (all concerned with sattwa, not tamas and rajas) grow stronger, he ceases to act with the motive of possession and enjoyment (cocoon making), and the result is that he comes out a butterfly, not the grub that he was when he dug himself or wrapped himself in. Such is destiny. Thus he operates in this world the three functions of creation, preservation, and destruction.

In overcoming the world he is overcoming his own past self, is working at his own resurrection, and is preparing for his own ascension. So, our verse says, let him rely upon sattwa in this present undertaking of realizing in consciousness that which is truly himself. Mentally he has wrapped himself in the false self idea, and now it is possible for him to come out of that mistake.

> *Verse 280.* Saying "I am not this living being (jīva) but the Life Beyond (Parabrahman)," and thus eliminating that strong desire-habit (vāsanā) previously produced,
> Perform the removal of your own mistake.

Comment. Here, in order to avoid another error — the idea of a Supreme God of an anthropomorphic kind when using the term Parabrahman — I have boldly translated the term as "the Life Beyond" — beyond all this, that is. This is well justified by the fact that *para* means simply "beyond" or "other than," and the word *Brahman,* although often thought of and translated as "God," comes from the verbal root "brih" which means to grow, and so means life, which is what in this world is that which grows. It is the para-brahmic influence or impulse in all life that makes it what it is seen really to be, the self-initiating creator of all forms, since matter is governed by forces and forces are governed by lives. Although still tinged with this anthropomorphism by this word "life," it is about the safest word we can use, as it affords at least an analogy in the relative world of action and language-communication for the absolute self-existent cause of itself and everything else.

The analogy is reliable for, as this verse points out, it is nothing less than that absolute which is stated by us when we say "I" to ourselves. It is but one more step in thought for us to admit that there is only one "I" in all of us. (Oh, what a concession and what a come-down to have to write "in all of us," since we are in it, not it in us!) Let us, then translate Parabrahman as the Life Beyond, at least in this verse.

This reminds me — for we must loosen up — of a story I heard about two Christians of different persuasion who were discussing the Trinity. One argued "But surely you can imagine three men in one cart?" The other replied, "Yes, but my difficulty is that I cannot imagine one man in three carts."

> *Verse 281.* Having come to know the selfness-of-all of oneself, by means of scripture, reasoning and one's own experience, somehow the shining (of the Real) arrives. So —
> Perform the removal of your own mistake.

Comment. These three modes of knowing are described in Patañjali's Sūtras as the only ways of getting right ideas about things, as distinguished from wrong ideas, fancies, dreams, and memories. Shankara goes further and makes it clear that only one of them — direct experience — is fundamental, as even testimony and inference depend upon that.

> *Verse 282.* For the sage (muni), then, there is no action — not the least — either of drawing back or of surging forth — that *ought* to be done. So with one-pointed intentness on That:
> Perform the removal of your own mistake.

Comment. What is usually translated simply as "the sage" is the "muni," which means the "silent one." He is "silent" because he knows that which cannot be spoken, because there is nothing else with which it can be compared and described. Even when he speaks he is really silent, because there are no words for it, and because — still further — there are no thoughts or mental images of it. The Zenists understand this, but even so they have been tempted to say that on an occasion when Buddha smiled significantly while looking at a flower, at least one of his disciples was suddenly illumined by that "communication without words." But even this will not do, for a gesture (a smile) is still in the same category — it does not, as such, convey the real knowledge to another. There is still silence.

> *Verse 283.* Arising from such great sayings as "That, thou art" (Tat-twam-asi) there is realization of the unity of Life and Self (or God and Self, Brahman and ātman). So, for confirmation of the Brahma-ness of the Atma-ness,
> Perform the removal of your own mistake.

Comment. Tat-twam-asi is one of the most often referred to and repeated of the great sayings of the Upanishads. There is a very famous story in the *Chhāndogya-Upanishad,* Chapter vi, in which a young man just returned home from twelve years' study at a place of learning is questioned by his father as to whether he had learned about the most important of all things, on which all else always depends. The answer being negative, and the son having requested information, the father explained that in the beginning or at first all this universe or manifestation was "one only, without a second," and that that one was Being. From that all else came forth, and yet all else is always fundamentally that.

The whole text is translated and explained in Radhakrishnan's *Principal Upanishads* (Harper and Bros., New York), and there he explains: "Tat twam asi; that art thou. This famous text emphasizes the divine nature of the human soul, the need to discriminate between the essential self and the accidents with which it is confused and the fetters by which it is bound. He who knows only what is of the body or mind knows the things that may be his but not himself. The text 'That art thou' applies to the inward person, antah purusha, and not to the empirical soul with its name and family descent."

Being is thus something in itself, and is the power by which all things exist. It is their substance, just as gold and clay are the substances of rings and pots. So Being is also God, called swayam-bhū, the self-existent, or the kaivalya, meaning non-dependent. We must not, of course, characterize it as emptiness, but rather as a fullness — a unity in which each includes all. Having taken this stand we can then say that all other than that — everything — is a lessening of *being*. Any manifestation is thus a lessening of the reality.

Every action has this character of lessening, separation, or disunity. "This summer we will go to London." Then you will not go to Paris. "But last year we went to Paris." But your memory of Paris as a thing of your past is not as good, as valid, as authentic, as "being," as your present experience of London, if that is where you now are.

In practice, however, we find this concentration on one thing after another to have the great value of enhancing our powers, whether of the body or of the mind. These enhancements or enrichments are then ours in the midst of all the future bits of being or living that we may perform or encounter. If last year I learned to speak French and enjoy reading in French, and this year I undertake to learn Spanish, my experience of Spanish will be all the richer for that past. The *quality* of my capacity in that field has been enriched. There is more "being" to it, more power.

Thanks be, then, for this system of bondage to "one thing after another" — which for us means the evolution or unfolding or opening up of our power, which is not an accretion but an actualizing of our potential, an increase of our power to be and our consciousness of that "being" that we essentially are.

Then, as in evolution progress is by steps up, so some day we shall step up from love (the capacity for living as others) into some spiritual consciousness of which the mystics and seers have given us some intimation, just as in the past there has been a step from the clod to the plant-consciousness, from the plant to the animal, from the animal to the cunning, thinking man, from the mental man to the loving man — and, in all this, never with a loss of what went before it. Love does not deny thought; thought does not deny feeling. Each step is a moreness in consciousness of present being.

Therefore our text tells us to use our will-power to the full in the day in which we now are. And this because our unfoldment is from within — not a gift from our environment, but a growth from what we do with it, in the field of the senses, of the mind, of love, and of what is beyond even that.

> *Verse 284.* Until there is a complete dissolution of this bodily I-being, carefully and with whole-hearted attention:
> Perform the removal of your own mistake.

Comment. At one time, in my Sanskrit class, in the course of the explanation of the use of various words, I had occasion to explain the meaning of the word jayami, "I conquer." I pointed out that this word was used not merely by a general who conquered his country's enemies, but by the old students of India with reference to their school lessons. They would not say, to take a modern example, "I learn algebra," but "I conquer algebra." There is a difference between the attitudes, "I will learn algebra," and "I will conquer algebra." The difference is in the psychological attitude — negative and positive respectively. Our present verse of the Chūdāmani (like many other verses) positively inculcates this positivity.

Verse 285. As long as the (wrong) idea of life-and-world asserts itself, like something in a dream, so long, O wise One, without any lapse:
Perform the removal of your own mistake.

Comment. We have come to the end of this set of nine verses all having the same refrain. The advice and instruction they contain is addressed to those who have understood the place of spiritual awakening, experience, and realization in our human horizon or outlook, and have resolved to self-evolve toward it.

It is well-recognized in India that most people are not attracted by this prospect. The present kind of a life is what they want, but relieved of pains and troubles and filled with pleasures — even if moderate pleasures. Their scriptures advise them to proceed accordingly in their present living — still insisting that their future circumstances depend upon their present actions (what is called the doctrine of karma) — doing no harm to others, and "pulling their weight" in the social organism, without strain and without worry. In this way, they are taught, they will make for themselves future incarnations into the kind of living they now enjoy to some extent, and envisage as enjoying in fuller measure as time goes on. The doors are open. The reiteration in the nine verses is intended as a reminder, and a warder-off of the tendency to lapse into carelessness of this important matter in the midst of complicated and insistent external demands on our attention. It also helps to counteract old habit. Hindus generally are fond of such reiterative meditation, and would perhaps say: "Read these verses every day for some considerable time."

CHAPTER 16

THE COMPLEXITY OF THE I

We come now to a series of verses which emphasize the importance of reflecting upon the real nature of oneself, and seeing which part of this complex person is you, which is clothing, and which is tools for your job.

> *Verse 286.* Giving no opportunity whatever for sleepiness, worldly importunities, outside communications, and forgetfulness (to control your mind during this inquiry), reflect upon the nature of the Self.

Comment. This means that it cannot be classed in any one of the four mentioned activities; it has not the nature of sleep, nor of any kind of outward stimulus, nor of language, nor of vacuity. What, then, is it? That is to be observed directly, not by any comparison, or similarity or difference. Such comparison would give only a mental definition, not the reality that it is found to be in immediate direct experience of it as consciousness — with its two sides to the world, receptive and active.

This duality of receptivity and activity is found in all living beings, however lowly, and in every one of our sheaths (coverings, garments, or equipments, or tools). Thus in the body we have the sensory and the muscular systems, and in the mind we have the observing and remembering systems and the thinking or constructively operative system.

So let me not permit the phenomena to take charge, especially the dense body, for what it wants is not what *I* want — either to receive or to do. As a product it is activated from the future — an inherent life impulse of expansion or enhancement (fed from a potential or fount of its own) other than any of its tools or bodies. So, as regards the body, beware: —

Verse 287. The body, made of secretions and flesh, was produced by the secretions of mother and father. Having rejected this (in the present undertaking) as like something outcast, become one who has achieved the brahmanic state.

Comment. The word Brahma is in this connection very significant. It comes from the verbal root "brih," to expand or grow. That is a word which describes life itself, for that is never content or at rest, and is in fact never something settled or fixed. On the contrary: —

Verse 288. Just as the space in a jar is in the great space which is all over and is never separate from it — consider (vilapya) the self (ātman) and the Supreme Self (Paramātman). Quietly, by means of that undivided beingness, be always in the silence (muni).

Verse 289. Being yourself your own self-luminous authority (or basis) cast out (from your thought of self) both the objective universe (world-egg) and the objective individual (the smaller lump), as like unclean receptacles.

Verse 290. Re-seating in the always-blissful conscious Self, the idea of I (now) mounted in the body, and (similarly) setting aside the subtle body (with its vitality and mind) be always independent.

Verse 291. Knowing "I am the Brahman" — in which there is a reflection of the world, like a city seen in a mirror — you will become one "having done what was to be done."

Comment. There is great significance here, for it is implied that just as the pictures in the world declare or express the artist who made them, so all forms in the world are expressions of the life-beings who have made them. The unitary power is shown in the fact that not one of these things can exist alone apart from the other things, and not one of these beings can have an independent world of his own apart from others.

Verse 292. That innateness of yours, which is real being, original, consciousness, non-dual, bliss (joy), formless and not produced (by anything else) — go to that, setting aside the false body as an actor puts off his disguise.

Verse 293. This which is *seen* by the selves of all is likewise illusive; so also the objective "I-am," because it is known (seen) to be but from-moment-to-moment. The experience "I know all" (i.e., each moment, one after another) — how can that be attributed to the momentarily-changing "I am" series?

Comment. Here we touch upon the discussion which raged in Buddha's time and still rages, about the changingness of the ego or self. Buddha said that everything that we know (including self) is changing, and that includes all that we know as man (which he catalogued as six-fold: body and senses, feelings and sensations, recognitions, tendencies of all kinds, mind and mental powers, and even the will).*

Still, Buddha could speak of being free, in the illuminated state, from all these and thereby full of joy, though he warned that this state of being was not rightly to be called even "being"; it was *nirvāna,* a negation or blowing-out of this

*Vide, Christmas Humphreys' *Buddhism,* Pelican paperback, pages 94-95.

flame of creation (kriya), including the six-fold list already given. So, said he, we must not use any word including the word ātman (Self), to describe the nirvāna, though it might be admissible to use the word freedom with great caution and in no relative sense. In all this idea we see that the author of the Chūdāmani is essentially at one with Buddha as to the idea of the temporality of the constructed ego, and as to the idea of *nirvāna.* The difference lies mostly in the use of the word "ātman," for Shankarāchārya uses the word "ātman" as it is found in the *Bhagavad-Gītā* e.g., where it is clearly associated with the word *nirvāna,* which clearly signifies the absence of limiting qualities characteristic of the "bodies" (or sharīras and koshas) which constitute the false ego. It will be useful now to bring together the *Bhagavad-Gītā* references for a little study. They are in Chapter 2 (verse 72), Chapter 5 (verses 24-26) and Chapter 6 (verse 15). In Chapter 2 it speaks of one reaching "the nirvāna of Brahma," or the "Brahmic-nirvāna."

In Chapter 5 the reference is to one who attains "the nirvāna of Brahma" and is then called also a "Brahma-being."

In Chapter 6 we find the description or reference is to "the supreme nirvāna which is My (the divine) state and is peace."

The word ātman, indeed, does not mean "self" in any ordinary sense of the word. This word, as is the case with all words used for communication, has to refer to some finite experience; but it is commonly used in a mystic context as indicatory and not descriptive. Some derive it from the verbal root "an," to breathe, move or live, while others regard it as from "man," to think or understand. Behind it is the conception of sat (being), chit (consciousness) and ānanda (the joy of life-being, as such). Buddha disapproved of any careless use of these words; the mystic experience being different from any previous concrete experience.

Anyhow, the from-moment-to-moment-changing character of the ordinary ego, or mentally visualized self, throws it out of standing as the real being which we are, quite as much in this Vedāntic outlook as in the view and teaching of Buddha. The aim or purpose of the teaching of both schools of thought is the same — to show people their common mistake about themselves and to tell them that they can if they will perceive (realize is a better word) the reality which they are.

In the next verse our author makes an attempt at direct statement of the nature of ātman, by bringing in the word "witness" or "observer" (sākshin).

> *Verse 294.* But the real factual fact (padartha) of "I" is the witness (or observer) of "I" in every case, even in sleep — on account of (our) seeing of the being (of it). Scripture says that it is in itself unborn (or unfounded) and eternal (for always). That inward ātman (pratyagātman) is not defined as being (sat) or non-being (asat).

Comment. We are faced here with terrific language difficulties in the work of translation. Our modern language is so based upon basic materialism of thought that when we want to say that something is really self-creatively existent in its own right and power (the word is "padārtha" in this case) we have to say it is a fact, or "factual," or "actual" or "real." Look at these words. Fact means something made. Act means something done. Real means powerful, and thus comes nearest to what we mean by padārtha — something fundamental or basic, self-existent and self-produced. But if we translate it as "real", people think we mean actual and objective. However, Shankarāchārya turns it round and over and looks at it from so many angles that we are forced to shed our materialism and admit not only that *life* can exist as such, or be itself here as such, but also that we know ourselves as such. The I has to look at itself as itself, not as an eye looking at an object, nor as an object looking at an I, but entirely without *any* subject-object connotation.

This is what the materialistic critic will no doubt call "mystical" experience. Certainly it is not sensuous experience, nor is it mental experience, yet it is the experience of every day of all of us humans, and presumably all the animals, and all beings, but we have been educated into clothing it physically and mentally: When we strip off the clothing, the materialist calls it "mystical" and "unreal." Perhaps it is well as in so many cases, to quote an Old Indian proverb: "Ripe fruit will not remain upon the branch." Let us remember, however, that the mystical is not the denial of the actual and the mental, but is a third kind of experience, which can illumine those, just as mind can illumine sensuous experience, and make it more valuable and significant.

> *Verse 295.* The knower (observer) of all the changes of the changing must be always unchanged or eternal. The play of mind during dream and sleep clearly shows again and again the unreality of those two.

> *Verse 296.* So give up the assumption of being in this bundle of flesh (body), also the assumption of being in any such bundle—both imagined by the intellect. Having understood (or realized) knowledge of the "undivided" — not deniable with reference to the past, the present or the future — realize yourself as the Self (ātman), the peace.

Comment. If one thinks of one's past, however different the body, or the mind, or even the false ego of that time may have been, one must admit that the same conscious experiencing Self was there. Look at a portrait of yourself at the age of three in the present incarnation; you must admit that that child's experience was *your* experience. Or look forward to yourself at the age of ninety in the present incarnation; again you must admit that that old man's or old woman's experience will be *yours*. Look forward to your future incarnations in any race; however different the body and the education of the mind in that future, it will still be you, the same you as you are now.

So, says our author in verse 296, you should cease to identify yourself with your body, also with the activities of it, which are only the qualities of the subtle body, which is the mind. The picture that this mind makes of itself and its body (gradually developed, confirmed and consolidated by the child after the age of about two or three) is responsible for the false ego which is foisted as it were on the nucleus of that being which is the real conscious Self or ātman.

After thus describing various obstacles and lures which attach people to the troubles of rebirth, our author comes out with a thunderous statement in verse 298, ascribing all this trouble to common egoism. This is tantamount to saying that we can now, if we will, choose the path of wisdom or understanding, or we can continue to learn in the hard way.

> *Verse 298.* There are other obstacles (also) which are seen to be causes of rebirth for a man. There is in fact one root of them (all) — the first modification (vikāra) which is the I-maker (ahankāra).

Comment. Two words here must be examined in order to clarify the position.

(1) *Vikāra.* This means a difference-maker, therefore any created or formed thing. The manifest universe is entirely

composed of vi-kāra. Here our verse speaks of the first vikāra. This means the first or most basic division in the undifferentiated absolute. Put theologically in one scripture it is said that God, the one, willed to be (at the same time and without destroying the unity) many.

(2) *Ahankāra.* The first vikāra, says our verse, is ahankāra. We are the ahankāras, the many. Aham means "I," the individual, and kāra means maker. (The *m* is sounded as *n* before the *k*.) Thus as parts of God we cannot be harmed by any secondary or subordinate vikāra whatsoever.

This individual is that which each of us knows himself to be, essentially. It is one's identity in consciousness, such that if I have a toothache and you have a headache, your headache is not mine and my toothache is not yours. This experience of self is there — and just the same — in the babe and the old man, in the victim of amnesia before and after the coming of his affliction, in the ancient Greek of 2,000 years ago and in his reincarnation today. It is just I experiencing my experience, and as such not to be confused with my "clothing and equipment" — bodily, emotional, or mental.

In earlier verses we have been over the Vedāntic analysis of the human being, which shows the outermost garment to be his physical body, the next his "vitality," the next his mental equipment (including desire, imagination, and reason), the next his "higher intelligence" or faculty for the recognition of other lives, and then, as the fifth, his mirror of self or egoism (ahankāra). By the first or outermost a man has material contacts, by the second pains and pleasures, by the third desire and planning, by the fourth contact and co-operation with others, and by the fifth his sense of self.

Inspecting this fifth (really the first) we find it to be "our consciousness" — a misleading expression; it should be "the consciousness that we are." We also say, "this is my being"

— another misleading expression; it should be "the being that I am." This is being; all the other four are doings and havings, that is operations of doing and operations of having or possessing.

Possessing is holding-on-to, or carrying, and so "possession and possessor are equal and opposite." Thus the possession possesses us; our attention is engrossed by it. This applies all down the line, through ego (*my* self), love (*my* others), thought (*my* knowledge and ideas), vitality (*my* pleasure and pain), and body (*my* body).

With this analysis as our guide, we should now be able to see what is going on here. The author of our text is trying to persuade us to look at this situation, and observe it directly in and for ourselves. He is not concerned with merely giving us information. These children that we are have wakened up, become interested, become involved, and now they must see the whole world as a collection of the havings and doings of the conscious selves.

In the next verse our author will refer to the ego in almost modern terms, as the "wicked ego" (the durātman ahankāra). As long as there is an I involved in this there is (1) a wrong idea of self and (2) a bondage. That being overcome, there is not bondage, but freedom in the midst of everything. So let there be no idea of *escape* from all this, rejection of all this — that indeed would be our Dr. Freud's "back to the womb" error, common as it indeed is, and present in much so-called idealism. The great man is he who is himself in the midst of the crowd.

> *Verse 299.* As long as there is any attachment of one-self (to anything) by this wicked ego, so long there cannot be even the least sign (or character) of abiding-in-liberty.

Verse 300. Freed from the grasp of ego, one realizes one's own nature, and is (then) unstained, complete, eternally happy and self-luminous.

Comment. Our author will now show that it is the application of any of the lower four "garments" to the conception of oneself that causes our failure to grasp the self (oneself) by direct experience. Even the most virtuous and exalted pictures of oneself as a superior person must come under this censure. So let there be no slipping-back in this matter, he says:

Verse 301. The belief "I am this (which is) in the body" which has been devised by the mind with extremely confusing darkness (ignorance). Only in the complete destruction of this (wrong idea) arises the state of the Brahmic Self without (any) obstacle.

Comment. Now, through verses 302 to 307, the author — through the simile of a snake with three heads and in other ways — reiterates the importance of ceasing this egoism, this identification of oneself with something in the field of relative existence, even if it be only a mental construct. One must simply accept the obvious fact of what one is and not start in again to clothe it even in "glories." Everything that we do can be done without this foolish doll-in-the-hand. For saving space I omit these repetitive verses, and conclude this part of our subject with the three verses which follow:—

Verse 308. So, having set aside the ego, etc., and attachment (rāga) being given up as a result of obtaining the highest thing, become quietly composed in Brahman, through experience of the joy of the Self (ātman), by the fullness of the Self, without separateness.

Comment. A brief comment on the exact significance of rāga will be useful here. Some have translated it as desire, others as attachment. In my *Practical Yoga: Ancient and Modern* I referred to it as "being colored by" because the word rāga means dye. We become dyed or colored by outward things. This is more so as we are more primitive or more animal and less so as we become more human. There is always this conflict between the lower and higher interests and motives in our lives and actions. It is important therefore that we should not be "dyed" from the outside, instead of judging all things and holding fast to those which are good. It is the difference between being positively human, valuing things according to their value for life — one's own and others' — and being as it were a plaything of circumstances.

Verse 309. If, even though rooted out, that powerful "I" again comes to life, even for a moment, springing up from the mind, it can make hundreds of products, like a rain-cloud in the sky in the stormy monsoon season.

Verse 310. Having held off the egoic enemy, one should give no room at all to the sense-lures by mental following of them. Such indeed is the cause of their existence. It acts like water to a fruit tree which is becoming dried-up.

Comment. In this verse there is an indication of the science of the relation between object and subject. The latter is the cause of the former. In other words life is the creator (or producer) of forms. This is so from the beginning, or rather as far back as we can trace. The life or consciousness gets a notion that such and such an activity would enhance its existence and enjoyment of existence, so it follows that such doing produces a form or a modification of the form it already has, that is, in the field of growth or in the field of action. Without that "interest" no organic being would respond to its environment; with that "interest" it adapts a little to its environment (if animal) or adapts something in its environment to itself (if human). In this way all known forms have been made, whether human or animal, and (more simply) even the plant and the mineral atoms.

To understand this we have to set aside the prevailing modern (really primitive) presumption that the minerals are without life. Quite to the contrary, there is no form without life, in this view. All the forms we know are "thous"; there simply are no "its." That being so, unity is not the destruction of multiplicity but of separateness.

In the advancement of this realization in a human being we find that antagonistic attitudes cease and that even enemies are seen as benefactors. Having seen this mentally, and thus removed attachment to separates and dependence upon separates, a human being may reasonably look within and discover himself as *life* — independent, free and happy *as such,* not in objective terms, but in himself formless.

In the psychological analysis called self-investigation one can begin with any part of one's currently accepted "self." Let us take a finger nail. "The finger nail is not myself; the finger is not myself; the hand, the arm, the whole body is not myself; the pain, the pleasure is not myself; the bed, the chair, the carpet, the room, the house, the town is not myself; letters, words, language, ideas, thoughts are not myself; loved ones and even love is not myself."

The ego (ahankāra) is the inmost or last of this series. It is well known that this ego can taint even love, and smirch it with self-righteousness. It would of course be a mistake to draw back from loving because one finds this taint, and it is some comfort to know that the mere (but clear) recognition of the presence of the taint is what chiefly removes it. Similarly, one should not draw back from living; one should not give up what is below in the sense of rejection or repulsion, for we are in the position of the artist who grows by his work. It is ours to make a perfect picture, a perfect person, however small. Quality, not quantity or size, is what counts. That will take care of our maturing, and ripening, and release from the tree. "Ripe fruit will not remain upon the branch."

So it is not "I" that is objectionable. It is the tainted "I" called ego. Without ahankāra we would be dead; but without identification with that false or tainted ahankāra which is the personal self-image, we can come really and fully alive. It has to be; it is part of our work, our product in the world, our artistry. But it is not "myself." This is what Shankarāchārya is telling us, and in this connection we have much reason to thank him for the books he left, especially perhaps the *Viveka-Chūdāmani.*

CHAPTER 17

The Significance of Desire

At this point (verse 311) our author Shri Shankarāchārya takes up the significance of desire (kāma) in human life, and we find him entirely in line with his predecessor, Buddha, in this respect. Desire, according to both these teachers, is the cause of objects or forms and also of our attachment to them.

We find ourselves in the midst of a situation in regard to both space or objects and time or actions. If we have built a house, there it is. It "occupies space," and if we want to keep it and live in it there we are, caught in that piece of space. This remark applies to all ownership. But now we have to add that action is also going on. We are not static beings or objects. We are alive, so there will be action with regard to that house. I can hold on to it, run away from it, sell or exchange it for something else, or alter it or give it away. Some of this I will certainly do, for my desire is never still — and that is so because life (which I am) is never still.

Extend this idea, and we can at once see that all objects in the universe are products of the desires of living beings. So here we all are in a seething mass of restless makings, exchangings and breakings of things. And then — each one of us is where he is because of his desire-relation to these things; including both desire to keep certain things in our grip (in our world, as we say) and desire to avoid other things.

We like the things which we find to be pleasurable and dislike those which we find to be painful. We all act accordingly, and so the kaleidoscopic whirligig goes on.

Both the teachers we have mentioned have expressed the same opinion about these things. They have said that the objects *do not bind us*. They cannot do anything to us, for after all they are only things or objects. But — and here is the rub — we bind ourselves to them by our desires.

"Well" (I seem to hear a voice, protesting), "what is wrong with that, if only we can have the things we want and avoid the others?"

The answer to this is seen in the boredom of wealthy people. They require ever new or more intense pleasure, and the reason for this is that they are *alive* and *growing,* and are discovering that the pleasure is in themselves, not in the things. The child outgrows its toys. The real adult is aware of himself as the player with the toys — not as the enjoyer of the toys but as the enjoyer of his own play with the toys. What would be the use of a set of chessmen to someone who does not know how to play? Of course, he could hire someone else to play chess for him!

And so in time we become very much aware of our *living* (whether physical, emotional, mental, or ethical). Further, in this process we become aware of factual limitations. We can do only a certain amount of jumping about or of eating. So we try to enhance these enjoyments by dashing about in motor-cars and by inventing new exciting spicy foods. But here we soon again strike factual limitations.

Still, in pursuing those things we find our knowledge and our cleverness becoming the main interest of our being. Here too the same result intervenes — there is impossibility on the quantitative side and incapacity on the subjective side.

This is where the teachers step in. They say, "Do not be such a fool as to involve yourself more and more in these creations and productions, but turn your attention to *living* and trying to discern what your life essentially is." They go further and say, "We ourselves have found what is present here and now and always, which is beyond bodily, emotional, mental, and moral living, and can and does pervade all of them." Then they warn, "So, do not be such a fool as to look for your happiness in particular things, and do not feel any dependence upon them, but be confident that the better living and the better consciousness will be yours as soon as you stop immersing them in this common error, and thereby putting yourself over and over again into this bondage by your own desire."

So now we find Shankara saying: —

Verse 311. The desirer stands there as a body-self! Without that character how could one be kāmic? Therefore it is only the following of attachment (of self) to objects which is the cause of bondage to what exists (outwardly), by attachment to those separates (things quite other than the self).

Verse 312. From the expansion of the effects (the objects), the operation of the cause (seed, or desire) can be seen. By the destruction of the seed (the cause, i.e. the desire), therefore, the effect is to be controlled.

Verse 313. From the expansion of desire the effect (arises), and by expansion of the effect the desire increases, (such is the vicious circle). In both these ways the circuit of material bondage (or reincarnation) is not decreased for the (real) man.

Verse 314. For the cutting-off of bondage to the circuit of material living the burning away of both these two is the means, i.e. both the desire and the effect (the objects), by thinking and by outward action (respectively).

Comment. Here I must remark upon the perspicuity with which Shankara points out *exactly* the cause of our bondage to things. It is the wrong idea of the "body-self," or self as body. It is as common today in our modern world as it was in ancient times. Although we glibly talk about having set aside "materialism" we still think of self as being dependent upon *some sort of objectivity*. Some people talk about "finer" bodies and "finer" planes, but they are still hag-ridden by the same old wrong idea, which makes them want to picture the life or the self as *something*.

We *must stop this* and understand that *life is life,* and is in no sense whatever dependent upon any real or fancied object, or matter. What is going on in this world is *action;* that action is in all cases the action of living beings — *of life* — and there is no such thing as anything actually static. Least of all must the life, the self, be thought of as something static—something static that is moving and acting!! This applies to the wrong idea of the *body-self* mentioned in verse 311, and also to the idea of the ego-self (well known to modern psychology) depicted as an entity having certain characteristics, for this again brings in a static and a dependency.

We have commonly no difficulty in thinking of matter as basic, because it seems so to our senses, but experience and scientific knowledge have disposed of that misconception. Yet the deeply-rooted habit remains. Why should it be difficult to believe and realize that life itself, including "our life," or rather the life that is ourselves, is basic? There has to be being, or else there would be nothing. Is it more difficult to observe that life is that being than that matter is that being?

I know it will be said that animals and plants and human beings, while responsible for the forms of their own bodies developed little by little in the course of evolution into the patterns we now see, are not responsible for the mineral and "material" substances, e.g., the varieties of chemical elements. But it is insisted here that we are not justified in drawing a line between living and non-living forms. The minerals have their specific reactions and therefore personalities, and they show great stubbornness in the maintenance of those characteristics. They show "will," if not thought and love, and must be considered in the small and the integrate, not in masses and aggregates.

However, leaving them aside, we are called upon to realize ourselves as *life,* and to observe ourselves as beings living, a term perhaps preferable to "living beings," since in using this latter expression we are apt to use the term "beings" with a materialistic or objective background.

No one expects it to be easy to set aside the old habit of thought and to realize ourselves as life or lives. It requires the use of acute perception of what is going on, and at the same time the setting aside of old habits and routines. Some help in this matter is given in verses 312 to 314. In those we are told that whenever we happen to catch either the objects influencing our outlook, or the desires attaching us to them, we must come down upon them severely and not allow them to govern our outlooks and our responses. We are to decide clearheadedly in all cases what to do in a given situation, and we are to do so not regarding ourselves as body-selves.

Still, besides the refusal to submit to the two bondages, Shankara now points out that we have still another weapon in our armory: —

> *Verse 315.* (First half). Being increased by both these (i.e., the desire and the dealings or actions) that (i.e., the tendency to "body-self") produces the revolving (reincarnations) of the self.

Comment. It is plain, is it not, that if one desires a particular possession, comfort, refuge or pleasurable experience there will be attachment to that by feeling and seeking, and one will "make karma," as the expression has it? It cannot be too emphatically affirmed that external objects have no hold whatever over us, and that only our own desires and actions attach us to them.

But now Shankara reminds us that we are basically in search of something else. In the course of evolution, due to the pressure of life for "more life" and "new life," we have gradually developed action-organs (hands, feet, etc.) and sense-organs (hearing, seeing, etc.), and then mind (and even reasoning), and even love (interest in "other lives"), and now we have come to feel the need of something more than all these. For the fulfillment of love we feel the need for something less separate and less perishable than the "you and I" of body-selves. We feel the need of something which the mind can think of as "unity," or non-separateness, but which it cannot visualize mentally because all its facts are separate things in the field of action and multiplicity.

As the coming "newness" will be experience of a new kind of being, people think of it as "mystical," which is logical if we understand the meaning of the word "mystical." Literally it means "with the eyes closed," and that means with the eyes of the mind closed. To be careful let us say that it does not mean that there must be the shutting of the eyes to the facts of this world of action (or world of making), or a closing of the mind to the relations and laws that it finds among them, but it does mean a perception or experience beyond and above them. From the point of view of action, senses, thought, and love it is new, just as there was a time when mind was something new and above the body.

So now Shankara comes out with a word to indicate (not to describe) where we must look for this newness. He says:—

Verse 315. (Second half) and Verse 316.

The means for the destruction of "the three" in all the states (waking, dreaming and sleeping), at all times, everywhere, and in all ways, is by perceiving that all is nothing but Brahman. It is by the desire for true being that the dissolution of those three is effected.

Comment. First we must see why three are now mentioned, instead of only two, as before. The two were (1) the desires, and (2) the actions, or wanting and dealing with things. Now there is the addition of (3) the cycle of incarnations. It is, however, the perception that all is Brahman that is important, as being the means of overcoming these three.

The mention of Brahman does not merely suggest the idea of depending on God in any ordinary Western sense of that term. To make this clear let me give the description of Brahman from Apte's Sanskrit-English Dictionary: "The Supreme Being, regarded as impersonal and divested of all quality and action; according to the Vedantins, Brahman is both the efficient and the material cause of the visible universe, the all-pervading soul and spirit of the universe, the essence from which all created things are produced and into which they are absorbed."

Why this long statement, and not simply a reference to some abstract principle or reality beyond the reach of body or conception of mind? The clue to this is given in the same verse in its reference to "true being" as the supreme subject of desire, which being sought and found is the means to the dissolution of "the three" causes of bondage.

What, then, is the nature of the search? It is to experience in consciousness that reality which is being as such. Anything which is in the field of body or mind contains some exclusion of this reality. If we say, "I am a man" we thereby affirm something material or mental, and in that very act deny or exclude this experience of *being*. *Being*, it must be remembered, is not mere passive existence. It is the *power* that makes itself, or makes being be being. Without this nothing else could be. This *in itself* we must come to know and experience with all the validity and reality with which we now say to ourselves that we know the lesser and very limited facts of body and of mind. This experience is to be realized, but it can be done only when our desire is detached from those two limited things, our consciousness being fully alert beyond or above those two limited areas. We must be interested in that. We must desire that. It is present all the time, but is ignored because of the lower desires of body and mind.

It is not stated that one *must* or *ought* to pursue this desire for higher or essential experience. It is only stated that if you want to get away from bondage this is the way, and the only way.

Most people at present enjoy their bondage and call it life. All they desire is a happier bondage than they now have. There is no objection to this. It only indicates that they have not yet reached human maturity. When that maturity is being neared, the real Face will begin to make itself known in consciousness, and then the desire will shift from the toys to the reality. It is no reproach to a child that it is a child, and it would be folly indeed for the child to live without its play and the enjoyment of its play.

Indeed it is the case that human childhood belongs not merely to the first period of, say, 21 years, but also to the second period of emotional maturing, and even the third period, of mental maturing. After that a balanced appraisal of living (i.e. of desires and actions) should be possible. One must allow, of course, for advanced persons—many of them—

who show and can follow a loyalty (considered to have been developed in former incarnations) to the newness even at an early age, and while the personal maturing is at the same time going on in the current lifetime.

This is an appropriate place for us to meditate on the nature of *life* as basic reality, not matter or forms as basic. The matter and the forms (what we think of as matter is really all forms) are creations or productions of the life that is going on. They are fragments of living crystallized into possessions. This is what is at the back of the doctrine of karma. Every one of these interests and creations is a lessness of the potential of life, is only temporary, and will be outgrown.

This being realized, and a view of life as basic in all this business having been attained, we are in a position to meditate further that the basis of our living is really the real life (beyond even mind) which we have been discussing, and then to see that this is also Brahman and our real Self, with a sort of secret motive of its own which will govern our outer lives when we consent to its doing so. Thus Brahman is all, as stated in verse 316.

> *Verse 317.* When there is the decline of (attachment to) actions there is the decline of thought (about them), and from that the fading of desires (for them). The destruction of (this) desire is liberation (moksha). That is called "liberation during life" (jīvanmukti).

> *Verse 318.* When there is the blossoming of the desire for the reality, there is the melting away of the desires relating to "I." It is just as in the strong increase of the reddish morning light the great darkness melts away.

Comment. Concerning the reference to the "I-etc." desires in this verse, we must remark that it is not the personal ego or self-image which seeks and obtains liberation, but it is the true I which obtains liberation from attachment to that false I and other things.

Verse 319. (To repeat) Darkness and the effects of darkness — a network of uselessness — disappear when there is the coming up of the lord of day (the sun). Similarly, in the experience of the joy of the non-dual blessedness there is no bondage nor any trace of sorrow.

Verse 320. Doing away with (the fields of) objectivity and imagination, and realizing the nature of the reality as a mass of joy, you should regulate your time in a harmonious manner with respect to externals and internals while still in the bondage of karma.

CHAPTER 18

The Usefulness of Remembrance

"Do not forget" is the theme of our next group of verses. Do not forget, that is to say, the real Self. It sounds alarming, but is really quite simple. The Self is our own consciousness *as such*. "Our own" is here a somewhat misleading expression. It sounds like something extraneous that belongs to us, like our purse or our hat. It would be better to say "the consciousness that we are." Then we see that both body *and* mind are only tools for dealing with the world or with others — they are not ourselves. If our purpose is to get plenty of pleasures for the body and the feelings, we are then being immersed in what is sometimes called the lower self, though really it is no self at all. If it is pleasures for the mind that we seek, we are then immersed in what may be called the middle self. Again, this middle self is really no self at all, although it is thoughtlessly called "myself" by most people.

It is not that the lower and the middle self are in any way despicable. They are tools, and should be kept strong and clean and available for use. Legs are for walking and arms for lifting, let them be clean and strong. The middle self is, of course, our common or ordinary egoic self-image. Once we have caught sight of this fact, we see *both* self and ego at the same time.

Let the self not be forgotten or overlooked at any time, our author warns:

Verse 321. Carelessness about loyalty to God (the god within) should never be. It is of the nature of death, said the noble son of Brahmā.

The reference is to the sage Sanatkumāra, a character appearing in the great Sanskrit epic, the *Mahābhārata*.

Verse 322. Than that carelessness as to one's own real nature there is nothing more useless to a thinker. From it arises delusion, arises also the conception of (the false) "I." From that there is bondage (to the world). From that there is anguish.

Comment. Through more than ten verses Shankara now gives illustrations of these effects, such as that of slime growing on a pond, and that of a ball bouncing down stairs. He repeats the warning against carelessness, and recommends attentiveness, leading to "the attainment of the greatness of one's own eternal Self." Then:

Verse 333. The striver, having cast aside his search in the unreal, which is the cause of bondage, should stand by the vision of the Self (Atman) only, affirming, "I am this myself." Having definitely experienced for oneself this position, one becomes happy. It takes away the misery brought about by the great ignorance.

Verse 334. Seeking in the external (only) increases this result, also bad habits (of mind), more and more. Having known this by discrimination, and having set aside the external, one should take care to be aware of one's own real Self at all times.

Verse 335. When the external (world) is under control there is peace of mind, and within the peace of mind there is the vision of the highest Self. In that good sight there is the destruction of the bondage to (external) being, and in that control of the external is the pathway to liberation.

Verse 336. Is there living (anywhere) a well-informed person, one who discriminates the real from the non-real, one who clearly sees the great benefit and the correctness of the sacred tradition (in this matter), and has a desire for liberation, who — like a child — will (still) practice dependence on the non-real (false self, and external objects), the means to his own downfall?

Comment. The answer implied in this is: "Very definitely not." The "non-real" is here all that error of supposing that one is dependent upon external things for one's being or happiness, or is dependent upon one's false-self or artificial ego-self-image for those two good realities. It is very easy especially to fall a prey to that self-image. Though, of course, we are at work on that self-image, and can develop our will-power and our understanding by making a good job of it, still it is the I which is doing the work; that is important, is it not? That true I is very easy to see, even in a moment's pause from the two errors (with the seeing that is being, not as in the field of objects, with its duality of one who sees and another who is seen). And then we are like the artist who observes the picture he is painting, who is aware of its good and bad points, who is forever altering it a bit and trying to make a really good job of it, yet who knows full well that only an essential excellence is required, not perfection and that when this job has become too confused and muddled he can drop it (by what is called death — death of the body in the world, followed by another piecemeal death of the false ego in the mind afterwards, according to tradition), and start on a new canvas (reincarnation) from the point he has attained. That this attainment of a mature human life and personality is the definite means to "overcoming" is implicit in the belief that a tiny child, or a cow, for example, cannot attain liberation. Herein lies the importance of will, love, and thought. Then from those arises the knowledge of being through the will, or unity with others through love, and of the real harmony of all things through thought.

That we do not have to wait for the completion of this job before knowing the Self as such is testified by hundreds of witnesses (including perhaps you, my reader), who have had glimpses or occasional very clear realizations of the true Self ("the true life kept from him who false puts by" according to Sir Edwin Arnold's expression of the teaching of Buddha in *The Light of Asia*).

By old habit the vision of the true Self is clouded over again and again, but there always remains a memory of it, and once it has been seen, a longing for it, even amidst the clouds, and moreover in that darkness, a radiance from the vision which is never again quite absent. That is why frequent or regular meditative attention to this is often advised — not to achieve withdrawal from our task but to help in overcoming the erroneous habit of darkness from the past, so that at last all will be one joy — both living and life. And let me add, from the ordinary point of view of material science, that it is just as easy to believe that *all forms,* even the mineral, are the creations of life (which we do know directly) as that life is created by forms (which we don't at all clearly or definitely know). Or, in other words, it is just as easy to believe that the life which we experience ourselves to be is the basis of all things as it is to believe that something called material (not very well known, nor easily definable as such except in an illogical circularity) is the basis of all things.

And now Shankara gives us a little picture of the state of affairs which is the opposite of clear-sightedness. He makes a definite statement of the contrast:

> *Verse 337*. For one who clings to the body, etc. there is no liberation, and for the liberated there is no egoism of body, etc. (This is just as) for a sleeping person there is no awakeness and for the waking person no sleep, because of the difference in character of the two (states).

> *Verse 338*. Having known oneself among the stable and moving objects, inside and outside, and having seen the Self as the basis, and having given up entirely the (false) personifications of that indivisible nature (the Self) – who thus stands by – the full Self is liberated.

> *Verse 339*. The cause of liberation from bondage is by (seeing) the Self of all. There is nothing greater than the being which is Self in all. When this non-attachment to the objective is established, through devotion to the true Self, then for him there is that state of being of the selfness of all.

Comment. Then, in verses 340 and 341 our author refers to the sages of the past and present, mentioning that they attained through the calmness and self-control implied in the foregoing verses. Finally he concludes this topic with a recommendation of patience and steadiness:

> *Verse 342*. Even well-informed people are not able to destroy the (false) "I" quickly when its power is high, except those who are firm in the non-planning meditation (nirvikalpa samādhi) inwardly. Those desire-impulses come from many, many life-actions.

Comment. Nirvikalpa samādhi is a poise of the mind without any material or mental aim. Yet, as all samādhis are, it is a state of most alert conscious awareness. And it is thus a gateway into new experience of life, beyond the old kind, a feature quite consonant with the deliberate self-evolution involved, as even our scientists agree, in man's next step. Let us remember that evolution goes by steps; after a certain maturity of one conscious state and power a new one is born.

CHAPTER 19

THE CONSCIOUSNESS WITHIN AND THE OUTER WORLD

We come now to a small group of verses in which what may be called the psychological processes as between the consciousness within and the outer world are explained. The first simple statement is that what lies between and connects these two — the inner and the outer — is what in modern thought we call the mind. It is thus that we see the mind operating in two ways, as dealing with the outer world by reception through the sense organs (hearing, etc.) and the action organs (hands, etc.) and dealing with the inner world (mind and beyond) through the reception of impulses of intuition and faith and also with obedience and gratitude. The last item is that consistent and frequent illumination which accompanies us and is so familiar that it is hardly recognized as such, though there it is; except where the mind yields itself completely to sense pleasure or to the imaginings of such.

The next item is given in two words which we have already encountered, which will now be described. These two are (1) *veiling* and (2) *projection*. In any moment when the mind is operating as governor in the veiling of the senses (in our outer world) it is easily seen that a choice is being made, and this is what is called the veiling power. You are perhaps sitting quietly looking through the window and noticing the collective picture in a general way, when something attracts your attention exclusively, perhaps a bird, perhaps the sun blinking on a leaf. Then the element of the mind swings into operation; the covers are removed from the mouth of the cannon of the mind and it starts its aggression upon that special piece of the world, that bird or those shadows on the leaf. On the one hand, so to speak, it tries to get to what I must call *moreness;* that is, to observe it more accurately, to take in more richly that which is seen and to probe, as it were, for other and unseen features of the object. So much for the receiving side of the transaction. Then comes the aggressive (projective) side. That is, perhaps, to catch that bird and put it in a cage so that one may, at pleasure, continue the process or the pursuit.

It is to be noticed that this attention to the bird is a choice or a selection among the many things that one can take and while it is an accentuation or concentration of attention with respect to that, it is a withdrawal from all the other things. It is this, in fact, which produces in our minds the phenomenon of "thingness" which is so consistently in our minds, what causes us sometimes – at the early stages of meditation, when reaching into the higher consciousness – to try to find that higher consciousness as being of some kind of "thingness." With us in the world all things are in flux and every so-called thing is only a point of focus for the moment to pursue this study of the nature of "thingness."

To return to the study of the two words, veiling and projection, we have now seen the meaning of the first of them. It is thus, when we focused our attention on the bird, we equally withdrew it from all the rest. It is this withholding (or veiling) which is of special interest just now, because we are trying to see that the greater (the infinite, if you like, though that word, too, is a veiling) becomes the finite, and the Self, which knows no bounds, seems to become this entity which is looking at another entity, the bird. This is the *veiling power,* whether to be regarded in its universal aspect or as operative in its smallest or mental operations.

We come now to the second word, *projection.* This follows upon the first — the veiling. Now the action organs are set into operation through what is called desire in the mind, and all the business of doing, even to the most elaborate and extensive human creativeness, has it as its source.

I have but to complete this small sketch of the two powers of the mind by saying that the two apply both in the realm of so-called inert objects or things and in the realm of what we call other living beings, "yous," around us. Action comes within the sphere of projection, hence creativeness of things or forms in the world, or of ideas in the mind. In the philosophy of our author, the mind is divided in this manner; consideration with respect to the things is called knowledge and with respect to the lives is called wisdom. *Manas* applies to the first and *buddhi* to the second, and quite often these two are translated into English as of the lower mind and higher mind or intelligence. I must say, however, that among Hindu scholars the term "the higher intelligence" is much preferred for the latter.

Taken together, then, these two (the veiling and the projection, which occur in both the lower mind and the higher mind) will be spoken of as the two components of *māyā.* "Māyā" is usually translated as illusion. This must not be confused with another similar word — delusion. In delusion there is nothing there; in illusion there is everything there.

We should observe, then, the operation of these two faculties, the veiling power and the projection power, in the small affairs of our individual lives and thus we shall become released from what is called the bondage in which we find ourselves. The Hindu or Buddhist idea is that nothing in the "māyā" can release us. There is no such thing as escape. We have to step out of it, we cannot say: "Stop the world, I want to get off"; we have to get off ourselves and leave that world including the personality or ego to its own devices. Hence a valuable practical effect of this truth about living is to believe in reincarnation; that we are tied to our projects and projections both psychologically from the inside and factually from the outside, the latter being expressed in the West as the law of action (karma) though our author would no doubt very much object to the word law in this connection and prefer the simple word action. It is action, our action, that of each and all of us. It is only that.

And now to peruse our present group of verses: —

Verse 343. The veiling power through its strength captures the man by the delusive I-idea. The projecting power, with all its capacities casts him out (into the world).

Verse 344. Unless there is the withholding of the veiling power completely, the conquest of the projecting power is difficult to accomplish. In this distinguishing of subject and object — it is clearly like milk and water — the veiling power perishes of itself, by its own nature. Then, if there is no delusion, there will be no projection.

Verse 345. Correct discernment, born from greater understanding, having distinguished the true fact about subject and object, cuts away the bondage of delusion created by illusion (māyā). On this account, for the liberated person, there is no more running around (re-incarnation).

Verse 346. The fire of discernment of the unity of the Beyond and the Here burns away the forest of ignorance completely. How then can there again be any cause for the running around in the case of one who has understood the existence of non-duality?

Verse 347. The perishing of the false knowledge on account of seeing the two foundations of things is the departure of the veiling and also the departure of the misery produced by the projection.

Comment. These verses have explained that when the "veiling" disappears (on account of discernment) the "projection" also ceases. This is logical in the development of evolution, since thought comes first and then action. This may sound rather startling, and would indeed be so if we meant by "thought" the forming of blueprints or indeed any mental pictures of external objects. Let us take an instance — the monkey, as an example. Once upon a time this animal, we may suppose, climbed into the trees to escape from enemies or to obtain food. And then it developed hands fingers, and thumbs. We are not to suppose that its veiling in this respect consisted of an idea of these appendages, but that there was a desire (veiling) and an effort (projection), which slowly resulted in the formation of hands, fingers, and thumbs. The same principle applies all down the line; even to the most elementary organism. There could not have been any evolution at all without the life element bringing in its desires.

Then, when it comes to man, we find such a development of mind that he can *picture* himself what he wants (within limits), and make plans and blueprints, and proceed to objectivate them. In all cases, low or high in the scale of evolution, the two operations (veiling and projecting) are thus to be seen in action.

Now let us examine projection more carefully.

Our author now states (verse 344) that unless the veiling power is impeded the projecting cannot cease. We must distinguish between "subject" and "object." We commonly call ourself the subject and the body and other "outside" things the object. There is a very peculiar phenomenology involved in this statement, and that has now to be considered. We consider that outside things which are known through the five senses are "real," which is what they are not, but only what they *seem* to be. Light is not light, color is not color.

Next it is very necessary to *distinguish* between "ourself" as subject and other things as objects. It is necessary to observe that objects are produced by the projecting power. It could be called the creative power. The body is the projecting power. Then, the mind is the veiling power in us, and this is what we commonly regard as ourselves, and this is what we build up into an ego (or personality) during a lifetime as a center of self-regard, self-respect and often even of pride.

We must note that this too, although we call it "the subject," is *not ourselves*. It is the machinery for associating us with *a portion* of the external. It is the veiling power, because it cannot deal with the *whole,* but is selective. Let us see this clearly. Behind it is the Self or Atman, which is our consciousness, which is what we *are* always. Yet we must not imagine that this is a "subject" in the pair of subject and object. The Self is not a new subject observing the old "subject and object" as a new object. It is the power behind them and the source of our life's impulses. But we must not speak of "my Self," but the other way round; the mind is, if you like, "the Self's me."

The next verse (348) tells us that this is the reason why a man should learn the truth about veiling and projection,

if he wishes to have release from the bondage of this whirligig or roundabout (*i.e.,* reincarnation). It is to be understood
that nothing but one's own desire (whether arising in body,
mind or self) for something in this circus can bring about
reincarnation. Karma does not do it.

After all this has been explained, someone suddenly asks:
"But what is the *purpose* of all this operation of veiling and
projecting and escaping? The answer is "no *purpose.*" The
very notion of "purpose" is a veiling, is itself the setting-up
of a veil, is *mental.* And yet, of course, if we think of "no
purpose" we have again made an exclusion and set up a veil.

The simile of "play" has been used in this matter to break
away from purpose. The spirit plays; it dances; to it all things
under the veil are musical instruments. We mind-bound or
enveiled persons have to reason with reason so that it will
yield first to love (i.e., recognize life) and then to the spirit
(Self). The spirit will come "like a thief in the night" but we
must clear the road for it.

CHAPTER 20

THE THREE KINDS OF KARMA

There are now many verses in this grand work of Shan-karāchārya's which give us the same great ideas over and over again in different light — though always poetically perfect.

As the reader no doubt knows, karma is something that happens to us because of something that we did in the past, not just recently within the scope of present activities. Thus there is no accidental experience; everything that happens to us is specifically related to us. We may go further, and surmise that it is specially useful to us, can we but detect its lesson.

So, as the old philosophers of India said: —

"... Each man's living
The outcome of its former living is."

There is the source of the idea of reincarnation. One could not think that children are being born into this world of trouble without any self-cause. If there is law and order in the world so that the thinking mind can grow, it would be a terrible infringement of justice if there were not a moral law by which the "heart" may grow. The best that could be said for a dying man is, "He never did any harm to others." And that would also be the best past for a newly born child.

It is not everybody who wants "liberation from the wheel of births and deaths" — only the philosophers desire that. Contrary to the philosophers' desire, the vast majority of people love and desire this kind of a life; but they want it to be far better, far less troubled, far less painful than what most of us have now. If there is helpfulness to others there is counteraction of old past karmas, but there is also the enjoyment of harmonious life with others — and that breeds love because it leads to the discovery that relationships of love with others, however mild, all lead to the discovery of the life in other selves, and are then found to be the happiest relations or possibilities in our human life. Far happier than the enjoyment of things is the enjoyment of life with others.

Well then, let us proceed to the three kinds of karmas:—

Verse 442. As regards one who has realized the truth about Brahman there is no running around (reincarnation) as before. If there is not this realization of identity with Brahman, he is still facing outward, as before.

Verse 443. If he reincarnates through the force of his old impulses (desires) — the desires become weak on account of realization of the actual unity with Brahman.

Verse 445. The external things still exist in the case of one devoted to meditation. The scriptures speak of this on account of its being seen that some fruit of action (or karma) has already begun (prārabdha).

Verse 446. When there is experience of happiness (regarding the objects) in such a case, it (karma) is called begun (prārabdha). Every result is preceded by action; never otherwise.

One kind of karma has now been listed — namely, the *begun* (prārabdha). It is well explained in many old writings. It is begun and has to "run its course." Thus in ordinary life one "catches" a disease such as influenza or smallpox; it then has to "run its course." Therefore you have a certain kind of body and environment already in operation as a result of past karma now begun to work, expressing itself, and that must go on until other karmas wipe it out. You are not going to work upon it with pleasure so as to prolong it or work upon it so as to change it into something else, which would make some new karma to be faced.

As usually believed, and indeed as taught in the Upanishads, this *begun* karma of the body causes delay in complete or perfect liberation as long as the body lasts, and even then only outwardly. Karma can operate only on karma. It cannot mar the perfect inward realization of unity with Brahman.

In Verse 453 we come to the first mention of the other two kinds of karma — the *stored (sanchita)* and the *coming (agami)*. It states that the begun karma can be too strong even for the man of knowledge if he has the least trace of enjoyment for it, but not so that which has been *stored* and the effects of new actions. These two are eliminated by the correct knowledge. It adds:

> *Verse 453* ... but those who stand always firm in the realization that the unity of Brahman and Self (Atman) are not affected by any of the three, since they *are* Brahman without attributes.

It will help to clarify all this if we now quote from my *Vedanta Dictionary* the item entitled: "Karma, the Law of." Here it is:—

> "As all objective forms are the product (or karma) of living beings, that is, are their projections (vikshepas, q.v.) based upon their ignorances (āvaranas, q.v.), and it is held that the producer is responsible in every case for his product; it is further held that he is, as it were, tied or bound to that product until he wipes it out by counteraction. This is held to operate always and everywhere, and so is called a law.

"Put in other words, didactically: 'You get what you make and nothing else, whether you make it for yourself or do it to others.' Thus who works for wealth or personal beauty (for example) will get precisely those, but he will also get the incidental effects of what he does to others while so working for them. As a consequence, each living being possesses quite a large collection of 'karmas,' and as he cannot attend to them all at once, just as he did not produce them all at once, they are — under the law — stored up (somewhat like 'potential energy' in modern physics) ready to discharge themselves upon him at appropriate moments, when he happens to provide the proper vacuum. This store is called his accumulated karma (sañchita karma).

"At the time of his taking a new birth a coherent portion of this collected karma provides him with his new conditions and circumstances (called jati). The portion of karma thus started whether at birth or subsequently is then called an 'undertaken' or 'started' karma (prā-rabdha karma), and this must run its course, or be endured and dealt with (somewhat as, e.g., one may perhaps say, a common cold, once contracted, must 'run its course'). There remains to be considered a third kind of karma — what is currently being made and paid by the entity (called kriyāmāna or vartamāna) This is sometimes called 'ready-money karma,' and is probably the most of our karma in daily life.

"It is further held that under the law only selfish actions (however subtly so) make this objective karma, and also that perfectly unselfish actions now being done cancel out corresponding portions of the 'stored' karma, so that they will never have to be met and dealt with in the objective world. There is a moral implication in all this — that since all that is done to others with selfishness, thoughtlessness or laziness (sins of omission) come back to the doer, the return of the same to the doer has educative value. On this account the law of karma has come to be called the law of justice and at the same time the law of universal goodness and kindness.

"The binding effect of karma lies not only in its nature of 'what you make you have,' but also in that it persists until you unmake it, or in other words 'work it out.'"

We will now continue with verse 454 of our text:—

Verse 454. For the sage who lives in the Self (ātman) only as Brahman, entirely free from the external things and their effects, there is no connection with the factuality of begun *(prārabdha)* just as is the case with ordinary dreaming and waking.

Verse 455. A man who has awakened stands there as his own waking self, not thinking "I-ness" or "my-ness" with reference to the dream-objects and the dream-body which were there.

Verse 456. There is no desire to keep those false things, nor that dream world. If there is, then he is not free from sleep — that is clear.

Verse 457. Just so also, living in Brahman as his own true Self he stands, not desiring anything else. But just as there is memory of the things seen in dreams, so does the Seer (or Knower) with reference to eating, etc.

Verse 458. The body was made by karma (every bit of it in the course of a long time) — so the *prārabdha* of it may be understood. Not so, as regards the Self (Atman); never was the Self produced by work or action *(karma).*

CHAPTER 21

LIBERATION WHILE LIVING

Although the remainder of the verses in this grand poem contain no new information or ideas, the repetitions are very pleasing to the Oriental ear and mind, which love to dwell on pleasant things, mental as well as physical. It would be beyond the purport of this book to translate all these here, as well as beyond the size of it, and beyond the interest of the occidental reader for whom it is intended.

I see, however, a few scattered words to which I would like to give a little further thought. Our author lays great stress on the task of passing in meditation from the objective and the subjective to the real (nirvikalpa samādhi). What do we mean by real? That which is the same in all things. Thus, for example, a black cow and a white cow each lacks something which the "perfect cow" would have — it would be both white and black at one and the same time. A still better example is "something" or "anything" compared with "nothing." Examples of "somethings" are all objects and ideas. An example of "nothing" is perhaps "space" — space is nothing, just nothing at all! But both are parts of the world of reality. We may say that both are real, but must admit that they are not really real, as *the* real is. There has been a separation-out from the real in each case — or some exclusion of it.

Well, then, the real samādhi is that which does not traffic in somethings and nothings. What then is there? Self, or pure consciousness, or "I" in the true sense of the term, as we actually (if we will) experience ourselves, without the addition of any mental affirmation, and equally without the negation of anything. The gate is open. Look right in!

First of all there is no objection to "hearing" the words of others, especially sages on this subject; secondly, this is followed by thinking on the same or on your own topics (mānana), and third, it is the stage of deep meditation (nididhyāsana).

Let me round it out, however, with two selected little groups or sets in which there is a recurrent theme which is very pleasing.

> *Verse 428.* Whose illumination is steady, while bliss (ānanda) is continuous, who hardly remembers the miscellaneous world — *he is called liberated while living.* He whose attentiveness is absorbed (on Brahman), withdrawn from the character of the waking state, and whose understanding is free from desires — *he is called liberated while living.*
>
> He whose interests in the whirligig (sansāra) are at peace, although having parts (body, etc.) is not sectioned, and of whom the thoughts (chittas) are without worry — *he is called liberated while living.*
>
> Affairs in "this body of mine" carry on like shadows, in the absence of possessiveness of "I-ness" and so *he is designated liberated while living.* Not brooding on the past, nor planning for the future, unconcerned with what is going on now — *he is designated liberated while living.*
>
> Because there is an absence of thought of "external and internal," because the mind being engaged in the experi-

ence of the bliss of Brahman — *he is designated liberated while living.*

He who is unaffected by what is to be done regarding body, senses, etc., and is free from "I" and "mine" — *he is designated liberated while living.*

He who has realized himself as of Brahma-nature, with the help of scriptural and philosophic writings and is released from the bondage of external "being," — *he is designated liberated while living.*

When there is no "I am" with respect to the senses, and no "it is" with respect to other things — *he is spoken of as liberated while living.*

He who on account of insight (prajña) never confuses the living being (mind and body) with Brahman, nor Brahman and the world (sarga or surge of evolution) — *he is designated liberated while living.*

He who remains the same whether in being praised by the good or in being blamed by the wicked — *he is designated liberated while living.*

He in whom the sense-objects projected out by others, lie down without effect like rivers flowing into the sea lie down — *that saint (yati) is liberated.*

The Vedanta doctrine sets forth that the whole universe and all jīvas (individual souls) are but Brahman, that moksha (freedom, liberation) is abiding in the indestructible essence which is the ātman; and the Shrutis (scriptures) are the authority for the non-duality of Brahman.

Thus comprehending — through the guru's teaching, through the authority of the Shrutis, and through his own reasoning — the supreme truth; he, the disciple, with organs of sense controlled, with composed mind and motionless body, remained for a time intent on the Atman.

Having fixed his mind for a time on Parabrahman, he then got up from meditation and said, with much ecstasy, these words:

Through the realization of the Atman with Brahman, my understanding is utterly lost and mental activity has vanished. I know neither this nor that, nor what this bliss is, its extent, nor its limit.

The greatness of Parabrahman, like an ocean completely filled with the nectar of realized bliss, can neither be described by speech nor conceived by mind, but can be enjoyed.

NOTES ON THE DATE OF SHRI SHANKARĀCHĀRYA

From the writings of T. Subba Row, B.A., B.L.

(Published 1910, Bombay, India, by Rayaram Tookaram)
It is always difficult to determine with precision the date of any particular event in the ancient history of India. In examining the various quotations and traditions selected by European Orientalists for the purpose of finding Shankarāchārya's date, special care must be taken to see whether the person referred to was the very first Shankarāchārya who established the Adwaitee doctrine, or one of his followers who became the *Adhipatis* of the various *Mathams* established by him and his successors. Many of the Adwaitee *Mathadhipatis* who succeeded him (especially of the Sringeri Matham) were men of considerable renown and were well-known throughout India during their time. They are often referred to under the general name of Shankarāchārya — consequently any reference made to any one of these *Mathadhipatis* is apt to

be mistaken for a reference to the first Shankarāchārya himself. . . .

It cannot be contended that the generality of Orientalists have any definite opinions of their own on the subject under consideration. Max Müller does not appear to have ever directed his attention to this subject. Monier-Williams merely copies the date given by Mr. Wilson, and Mr. Weber seems to rely upon the same authority without troubling himself with any further inquiry about the matter. . . . Mr. Wilson is probably the only Orientalist who investigated the subject with some care and attention; and he frankly confesses that the exact period at which "he (Shankara) flourished can by no means be determined" (page 201 of vol. 1 of his *Essays on the religion of the Hindus*). . . .

Mr. Wilson writes as follows: — "The Kadali Brahmans who form an establishment following and teaching his (Shankara's) system, assert his appearance about 2,000 years since; some accounts place him about the beginning of the Christian era, others in the 3rd or 4th century after. . . . The Bhoja Prabandha enumerates Shankara among its worthies, and as contemporary with that prince; his antiquity will then be between 8 and 9 centuries. . . . The Vaishnava Brahmans of Madura say that Shankara appeared in the ninth century. . . . Dr. Taylor thinks that if we allow him 900 years we shall not be far from the truth, and Mr. Colebrake is inclined to give him an antiquity of about 1,000 years. This last is the age which my friend Ram Mohun Roy, a diligent student of Shankara's works, and philosophical teacher of his doctrines, is disposed to concur in, and he infers that "from a calculation of the spiritual generations of the followers of Shankara Swami from his time up to this date, he seems to have lived between the 7th and 8th centuries of the Christian era, a distance of time agreeing with the statements made to Dr.

Buchanan in his journey through Shankara's native country, Malabar. . . ."

Max Müller fixed the Sūtra period between 500 B.C. and 600 B.C. . . . Patañjali was the author of the Yoga Sūtras, and this fact has not been doubted by any Hindu writer up to this time. . . . As Shankarāchārya was a contemporary of Patañjali he must have lived about the same time. . . . As we have shown that Shankara was Patañjali's chela and that his date should be ascertained with reference to Patañjali's date. . . .

Shankara was born in the year B.C. 510 and we believe that satisfactory evidence in support of this date can be obtained in India if the inscriptions at Conjevaram, Sringeri, Jaggarnath, Benares, Cashmere and various other places visited by Shankara are properly deciphered. Shankara built Conjeveram, which is considered as one of the most ancient towns in Southern India. As Goudapada was Shankarāchārya's guru's guru, his date entirely depends on Shankara's date; and there is every reason to suppose that he lived before Buddha.

— Compiled by Hilda Wood

Note: Ernest Wood died September 17, 1965, four days after finishing the translation of *Viveka Chūdāmani*. He asked me to add these notes regarding the time of Shankarāchārya's birth. — H. W.